She had seen him angry before but never like this. It flashed through her mind how she'd persuaded him to come against his better judgement, and she saw clear as light the trap into which she'd fallen. Knives and forks were still. Jaws dropped.

Only Sheila Bissett moved. She was draining the last dregs of her wine. When she put down her glass, she looked around the table. 'You'd be glad to help, wouldn't you, Sir Ralph? You both remember, don't you?'

Educated at a co-educational Quaker Boarding School, Rebecca Shaw went on to qualify as a teacher of deaf children. After her marriage, she spent the intervening years enjoying bringing up her family. The departure of the last of her four children to university gave her the time and opportunity to write. Her study window overlooks the Grand Union Canal from which she can watch the very varied canal life. She enjoys gardening, walking, feeding her swans and going to the theatre, but finds her writing leaves little time for leisure pursuits.

BY THE SAME AUTHOR

The New Rector
Talk of the Village
The Village Show

Village Matters

REBECCA SHAW

PHŒNIX

A PHOENIX PAPERBACK

First published in Great Britain
by Orion in 1996
This paperback edition published in 1997
by Phoenix, a division of Orion Books Ltd,
Orion House, 5 Upper St Martin's Lane,
London WC2H 9EA

A CIP catalogue record for this book
is available from the British Library.

ISBN: 1 85799 851 0

Printed and bound in Great Britain by
The Guernsey Press Co. Ltd,
Guernsey, Channel Islands

INHABITANTS OF TURNHAM MALPAS

Barry's mother	A village gossip.
Sadie Beauchamp	Retired widow and mother of Harriet Charter-Plackett.
Sylvia Bennett	Housekeeper at the rectory.
Willie Biggs	Verger at St Thomas à Becket.
Sir Ronald Bissett	Retired trades union leader.
Lady Sheila Bissett	His wife.
James Charter-Plackett	Owner of the village store.
Harriet Charter-Plackett	His wife.
Fergus, Finlay and Flick	Their children.
Alan Crimble	Barman at The Royal Oak.
Pat Duckett	School caretaker.
Dean and Michelle	Her children.
Bryn Fields	Licensee of The Royal Oak.
Georgie Fields	His wife.
H. Craddock Fitch	New owner of Turnham House.
Jimmy Glover	One time poacher and ne'er do well.
Revd. Peter Harris (MA Oxon)	Rector of the parish.
Dr Caroline Harris	His wife.
Alex and Beth	Their children.
Jeremy Mayer	Manager at Turnham House Training Centre.
Venetia Mayer	His wife.
Michael Palmer	Village school headmaster.
Sir Ralph Templeton	Retired from the Diplomatic Service.
Lady Muriel Templeton	His wife.
Vera Wright	Cleaner at nursing home in Penny Fawcett.
Rhett Wright	Her grandson.

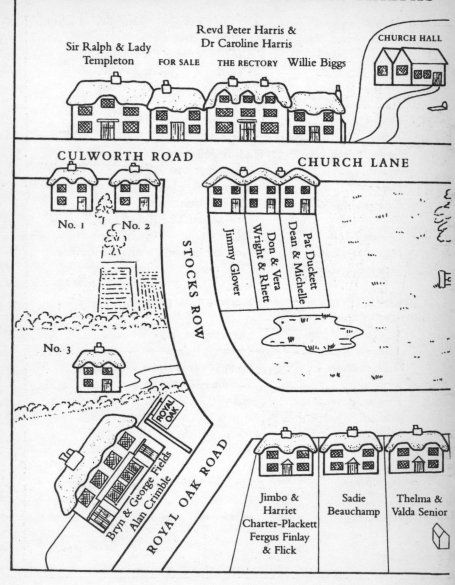

THE VILLAGE OF TURNHAM MALPAS

Revd Peter Harris &
Dr Caroline Harris

Sir Ralph & Lady
Templeton

CHURCH HALL

FOR SALE   THE RECTORY   Willie Biggs

CULWORTH ROAD

CHURCH LANE

No. 1   No. 2

No. 3

STOCKS ROW

Jimmy Glover

Don & Vera
Wright & Rhett

Pat Duckett
Dean & Michelle

ROYAL OAK

ROYAL OAK ROAD

Bryn & George Fields
Alan Crimble

Jimbo &
Harriet
Charter-Plackett
Fergus Finlay
& Flick

Sadie
Beauchamp

Thelma &
Valda Senior

Chapter 1

Peter shivered in the cold morning air. His prayers finished he got stiffly to his feet, stood back from the little altar in the war memorial chapel and crossed himself. At seven o'clock on a spring morning the church was certainly chilly. The old mediaeval stone walls kept the church cold right through the year, even in the hottest summer.

He went to stand in front of the main altar and looked around his church. Soon he'd have been in Turnham Malpas two whole years. When he'd first come here he hadn't realised how attached to the place he would become. He loved the deep colours of the stained glass windows, the ancient tombs slumbering there through the centuries, the banners, withering away at their posts for almost as many years, and the lovely country graveyard which was as much a part of St Thomas à Becket as the church itself. Still treading the village paths were people whose ancestors had for generations rested so peacefully within the precincts of this consecrated place. There was an ongoing feel about a village church, stretching back through the years and on into the future with an amazing sense of permanence. A city church didn't have quite the same feel about it.

He began to add up all the things he had achieved since his arrival. The Rectory cleaned and decorated and modernised and refurnished, the Scout troup, the Brownies and Girl Guides, the Luncheon Club for the pensioners, the women's meeting, the play group . . . for a moment his face clouded. The play group. That brought Suzy Meadows to mind. She'd still perhaps have been here running it if they . . . But they had and they shouldn't have. He still couldn't avoid the pain somewhere around his diaphragm. It knifed deep into his gut when he thought of her. No, it wasn't the thought of *her* as such, it was the thought of the crushing pain he'd inflicted on his darling Caroline which caused his agony. When she'd begged him to adopt the twins Suzy had given birth to because of him, he had thought he would die of it. But now he'd only to see their beaming smiles, feel their tiny hands grasping his, feel their soft sweet flesh against his own, and he knew Caroline had been right. It was the only course open. They were his, after all.

He glanced at his watch. Time he was off.

Peter's running shoes made no sound as he marched purposefully down the aisle to the main door. He carefully locked it behind him, checked it was secure, and then stripped off his tracksuit and placed it in a plastic carrier bag he kept for the purpose, under the bench in the porch. Underneath he wore his old college running vest and a pair of navy rugger shorts. He hid the huge key beside the grave he and the verger, Willie Biggs, had decided upon, and set off down the path. Jimbo Charter-Plackett was limbering up by the lych gate. Jimbo had been running with him for some time now and the flab he'd been anxious to lose was beginning to go. He was still a less fit looking man than Peter, for Jimbo was older, shorter, rounder and going bald: in contrast Peter was a good six inches taller, with an excellent head of blond hair, and an athlete's physique.

'Morning Peter. Lovely fresh day, isn't it?'

'Morning Jimbo. It surely is.' The two of them did their stretching exercises together and then at a nod from Jimbo they set off down Church Lane, then right into Jacks Lane and onto the spare land. Half way round their three-mile circuit was a five-barred gate where they always stopped for a chat. It led into a huge field and from it they had a view of Sykes Wood. It was a vast ancient wood, once part of a king's hunting forest, but belonging to Turnham House for the last three hundred years and possibly more. To one side where the trees were not quite so tall, the chimneys of the Big House could just be seen. After he'd wiped the sweat from his forehead with the hem of his running vest, Peter nodded towards them.

'Catering contract working out OK then, Jimbo?'

'It is. At least the money's more reliable than it was when it was the Health Club. Fitch plc certainly pays up on the dot, thank goodness.'

'Nice chap, is he?'

'Like all chairmen of big companies he thinks the world revolves round him, and his word is law, but as he knows I was a City man myself I do get a bit of respect for my opinions. They certainly do a good job with their staff training up there. Cracking computer equipment, video, cinema stuff and the rest. Technology gone berserk. That Jeremy Mayer's strutting around throwing his weight about, completely forgetting how grateful he should be that he's managed to sell on to Fitch and still keep a roof over his head.'

'What does Venetia do?'

'Mrs Venetia Mayer organises the leisure time for the

3

staff, and Mrs Venetia Mayer organises diversions in the leisure department for the chairman of the company I think, but don't quote me. I've a soft spot for Venetia despite her permanent come-hither look.'

Peter laughed. 'Come on then, I've got school prayers at nine, must get back.' They turned to go, Peter leading the way.

Jimbo followed on, thinking about his jobs for the day. First, on his way home, he'd stand outside his Store and appraise the window displays. Each window had to be changed alternate weeks. Thinking up new ideas for them was a pain, but it was one of his rules. It had to be done. No fly-blown displays with bleached crepe paper hanging loose for Jimbo. Oh no! That kind of thing belonged to the 1950s, not the 1990s. Just recently with the opening of the training centre at Turnham House there'd been quite a few young trainees in, spending their money, another boost to the profits, and summertime was always good, his sales curve went ever upward with the money spent by the visitors to the church and the old stocks on the green. In fact all told, this year looked good. The mail-order business was booming, due to some clever advertising thought up by Harriet, his outside catering was also booming and the Store itself, the hub of it all, was also doing better than he and Harriet could ever have imagined.

What next could he turn his hand to, to make money? By Jove he was going to need it, with this new baby on the way. He gave a skip and a jump when he thought about the baby. Not bad for a forty-one-year-old chap. Number four. And Harriet so well, and he'd keep her that way. More help. Yes, he'd need more help. Peter turned round to wave and continued on to the rectory, Jimbo nodded and turned down Stocks Row and round the green to his house.

The windows! He'd forgotten the windows. He turned back and went to stand outside his Store. Easter. Easter. Fluffy chicks. Yellow ribbons. Chocolate eggs. A raffle? Huge great egg as the prize. That'd bring 'em in. Just get them in and they'd be buying other things beside the raffle tickets. Twenty-five pence each and five for a pound. Maybe twenty pence each, six for a pound, some of the villagers weren't that well off. He'd work out on his calculator how many he'd have to sell to break even, and then decide. Full of ideas he was this morning. Full of 'em.

'It's only me! Harriet!' The front door slammed shut. He stood, leaning on the hall table trying to get his breath. Sweat was pouring off his face and he wiped it with the sweat bands he wore on his wrists. Flick had bought them for him for Christmas. His dear little Flick. She came dancing down the stairs at that moment.

'Hello, Daddy, I'm not going to kiss you, you're all smelly and disgusting.' She wrinkled her nose and headed for the kitchen. 'Mummy! Daddy's back. You boys hurry up, your porridge is ready.' Flick seated herself at the table and watched her two brothers pretending to box. 'Men do find some funny things to entertain themselves with, don't they, Mummy?'

Harriet laughed. 'They certainly do!' She glanced up and saw Jimbo grinning at her from the doorway. 'Quick Jimbo, get under the shower – I can smell the sweat from here.'

'Thanks a million! A chap's doing his best to keep fit and his womenfolk do nothing but complain.'

'I've been thinking about an Easter raffle.'

'So have I. Great minds!'

'Boys come along now, that's enough. On your chairs. Look, Flick's already seated.'

'Trust her.' Finlay shouted as he dodged another blow from Fergus.

'Miss Goody Two Shoes! Miss Goody Two Shoes!'!' Fergus danced around the back of Flick's chair tormenting her. Tears began to well in her eyes and Harriet put a stop to the teasing.

She indicated his chair with a sharp finger. 'Enough. Thanks. That's enough! Sit down and eat.'

By the time Jimbo came downstairs the children had disappeared to clean their teeth – or so Harriet hoped – and he sat down to his bowl of muesli, his orange juice and wholemeal toast.

'Coffee or tea this morning?'

'Tea, please. I thought about a huge Easter egg for the first prize.'

'So did I. We get on remarkably well together in business, don't we Jimbo?'

'Yes, we do. And we don't get bored with each other. It would be so easy to be bored to death seeing each other at work *and* at home. Feeling OK?'

'Of course. I've never felt better than this time. Linda has another appointment at the dentist's tomorrow. Will you manage?'

'Yes, I expect so. Hope this is the last one for a while.'

'It is, the poor girl can't help an abscess, can she?'

'No, I suppose not. More tea, darling, please. I'm going up to the Big House this morning, just to keep an eye on things. Will you be around?'

'As ever.'

Jimbo stood up from the table. 'I'm off then. Don't overdo it will you, Harriet? I couldn't bear it if things went wrong.' Harriet stopped clearing the table and took time to look at him intently. 'You're all I've got, you know,' he said.

She reached across to kiss him. 'I know. I know. Believe me I will take care, but I mustn't be mollycoddled. That's not my scene.'

'See you then.' He went to the foot of the stairs and called up. 'Daddy's going now. Bye you lot.'

Flick shouted downstairs, her voice impeded by her toothbrush. 'Bye Daddy, have a nice day.' Jimbo winced at the Americanism. 'Bye now. See you later, Harriet.'

'OK.'

The weather was good for the time of year. Jimmy Glover's geese were out and about as usual. They were grazing close to the edge of the green. He wondered if it was true that they were as good as a dog for protecting their owners. They looked remarkably relaxed this morning. But as he came closer and paused to watch them, the geese began to stretch their necks and honk menacingly. Two of them left the grass and came onto the road, their beaks, on a level with Jimbo's knees, opened threateningly. He shouted and skipped a few steps to avoid them, waving his arms; they lost interest and left him to press on. Blessed geese, if he had his way . . . Then he caught sight of his Store and his heart swelled with pride. He'd turned it round and no mistake. He remembered the depressing aspect of it when he and Harriet had first come to Turnham Malpas to view it. They'd looked at each other and mouthed 'No', but old Mrs Thornton had noticed, and they'd felt obliged to show some interest.

At the time the shop had been Mrs Thornton's front room. The stock was almost non-existent, the trade negligible. But once they'd realised that the cottage next door was for sale too, Harriet had grown enthusiastic. Now look at it. Jimbo took the keys from his pocket and opened up. He picked up the bundle of newspapers from the shop doorway, moved the two advertising boards out onto the tarmac, checked to see that the litter bin by the seat he'd provided wasn't overflowing, noticed the telephone box needed a clear out, and then entered his domain.

Quarter past eight. He was late. It was half an hour before Linda would come to open up the post office section, so after he'd laid the newspapers out on their shelf ready for sale, he decided to begin collecting Easter eggs and all the paraphernalia he needed for dressing the window. Scissors, measuring tape, sellotape, drawing pins, stapler, ribbons, yellow and white crepe paper, silver paper. First, though, he'd dismantle the current display. But his plan was thwarted, his first customer entered. The little brass bell jingled furiously.

'Morning Willie. Come to collect your paper?'

'Yes.' Willie went to help himself. Took it to the till and handed Jimbo the exact money.

'Keep thinking we shall be hearing wedding bells for you, Willie, but you don't seem to have set a date, or have you?'

'Sylvia and I are taking our time about it. We're not in a great bursting hurry like we would be if we were younger.'

'Well, there's one thing being the verger, you won't have any problems making the arrangements. Will Sylvia keep working at the rectory?'

'Oh yes, she enjoys that job, much better than at the hospital. Mrs Rector couldn't manage without her, not yet. I'll be off, rector's got all sorts of plans for Easter so we're having a conference today.' Willie went briskly out, leaving Jimbo confident that Willie knew exactly when he was getting married but he wasn't saying.

Arranging the windows was very therapeutic for Jimbo and he rapidly became absorbed in his work. The bell jingled again and in came his three children.

'Daddy, it's only us. We've come for something for playtime.' Jimbo reversed out of the window and went to supervise their choices. They were never allowed simply to help themselves, they always had to pay for whatever they chose. His mother-in-law laughed at his insistence on the matter, but he knew he was right. 'That's twenty-three pence for you Fergus, twenty-two for you Flick, and thirty, thirty? for you Finlay. That's a bit excessive isn't it?'

'Well, Daddy, we should really be getting them for free you know, it is our shop.'

'I'm not debating that question this morning Finlay, we've had it all out before. Out! Out!'

As they went out his mother-in-law, Sadie, came in. 'Bye darlings, be good.'

'Bye Grandma!'

'Good morning Jimbo. That word "Grandma" makes me wince, I start fumbling for my pince-nez.'

'You're early.'

'Do I detect a hint of sarcasm there?'

'No, no, not at all, but you are!'

'Well, I've lots to do today. Being in charge of the mail order doesn't give me much time to spare. Did that woman come with the jars of marmalade yesterday? She promised she'd have them made by Thursday last week.'

'Yes, she did.'

'Thank God for that. I hate letting our customers down. I'll have coffee when you're ready.' Jimbo groaned. He'd never get the window started. He began refreshing the coffee machine he kept in constant readiness for his customers. Just as he switched it on the door burst open and in came Pat Duckett from the school. Under her coat she had her school cleaning apron on, and her thick hair was standing on end, almost as though she'd used her head on the school hall floor, instead of her polishing mop. In her hand she clutched the school keys.

Pushing back her hair she whispered, 'Mr Charter-Plackett! Have yer got a minute? I haven't slept a wink all night for worrying. Can we go in the back where we won't be 'eard?'

'Heavens above, Pat, what's the matter?'

'It's that Mr Fitch, yer know, Mr Fitch plc? He's stealing the church silver and I don't know what to do about it.'

Chapter 2

Jimbo took her into the store room at the back and sat her on his stool. He removed his boater, and laid it on a nearby shelf. Seating himself on an empty mineral-water crate, he said. 'Now what's it all about?'

'Well, yer know I went up to the Big House last night to 'elp out, with that waitress being off with the 'flu? Well, there was a right flap on. 'Ave to admit I made it my business to find out, 'cos I'm a bit of a nosy Parker like you are.' Jimbo began protesting but then admitted to himself he did like to hear all the latest gossip.

'Apparently,' Pat took a deep breath, 'apparently they'd been doing some more alterations. Don't know if you've 'eard but Mr Fitch is 'aving some rooms done up for a private flat for himself, anyway this room he fancied for a sitting room, he calls it 'is drawing room but we all know it's where 'e's going to sit, he starts examining the panelling. Beautiful it is, really old, bit of woodworm here and there and he wanted to get it done. Starts tapping the panelling and finds that one bit sounds 'oller.'

'Oller?'

'Yer know, no wall at the back, empty like. Anyway

when 'e stands back to look 'e sees that that piece of panelling is a bit different from the rest, as if it 'ad been put in later. Course, he couldn't bear, 'as to have a look. Well, he gets the carpenter to remove this piece of panelling and lo and behold there's like a small room. An alcove thing. No windows, just a space and there, low and behold in cardboard boxes, stuff wrapped in old newspapers. They drag 'em out and believe it or believe it not it's all old silver things in there.'

'Whose silver things? Sir Ralph's?'

'I'm just coming to that. Apparently he gets unwrapping the newspapers and finds communion cups, two big silver plates, for like propping up on the altar, a pair of beautiful candlesticks, wonderful ones, and one that big, when the pieces are fixed together it stands on the floor. All really old. Well, he looks at the dates on the newspapers and they're dated June 1940!'

'June 1940?'

'June 1940. Yes, but, and 'ere's what's up, he says he's bought the house so they belong to him and he's going to sell them to help with the cost of his alterations!'

Linda came in. 'Hi! Mr Charter-Plackett, just wondered where you were. I'll carry on.'

'Yes, thanks, Linda. Won't be a minute.' Bemused, Jimbo didn't answer Pat for a moment. Had Fitch got a point here? He had bought the house, did everything in it belong to him? But church silver, he could hardly sell it. Could he?

'Look Pat, I've got to get on, there's only Linda and me this morning till Harriet gets here. Keep all this under your hat. Come back at lunchtime after you've finished at the school and we'll have another talk.'

'But it could be urgent. Yer know what a go-getter 'e is,

it could all be sold by tonight. Then what would we do? The rector's going to be none too pleased, is he? What I can't understand is why it's there in the first place. Why isn't it in the church?'

'I don't know, Pat.' He stood up to retrieve his boater from the shelf. 'Look, I still think we've got time. I'm due up at the Big House later this morning, I'll have a scout around and see what I come up with. Leave it with me.'

'Will you tell the rector?'

'Or perhaps we should tell Sir Ralph, after all his family still owned it in 1940 didn't they?'

'Did they? Yes, I expect they did. I'll call after I've washed up the dinner things. Right?'

'Right!'

'See yer then. Yer can understand why I'm worried, can't yer? If the village finds out what he's done there'll be hell to play.'

Jimbo placed his boater at a jaunty angle and led the way into the front shop. Linda was trying to serve and deal with the post office too, so for the moment he had to put the whole story to the back of his mind.

Jimbo dropped down to third gear as he went up the long drive to Turnham House. He loved sauntering up the drive, taking in the feel of the place. It mattered not one jot that it had been a children's home then a health club and now a training centre, the old house with its parkland and gardens still had dignity and beauty. Try as they might, the twentieth-century entrepreneurs hadn't spoilt that ambience. One mile long, exactly. He'd measured on his milometer. As he rounded the last curve the lovely old red-brick house came into view. The Big House. Even the village people who hadn't been born when Sir Ralph's mother had to sell because of Ralph's father's death in the War, still looked upon it as the hub of the village. He drew to a halt on the freshly laid gravel at the front of the house and, climbing out, left the car unlocked and went inside. Give him his due, Fitch had retained the lovely entrance hall in its entirety, and had had the sensitivity to place an antique desk for the receptionist to use.

'Mr Charter-Plackett! What a delight! How are you this bright morning?'

'All the better for seeing you, Fenella! What news on the Rialto?'

'You haven't heard then? No, of course not, you weren't up here yesterday.' Fenella's large blue eyes glowed with intrigue. She glanced round the hall, checked no one was within hearing, and leaning across the desk whispered: 'Buried treasure! Well, not buried exactly, but hidden!'

'Fenella, you've been watching too many late-night movies, I've warned you before.'

'Cross my heart and hope to die.' Jimbo took her hand in his. Holding it close to the revers of his Jaeger overcoat he said, 'Tell me more.'

'All the stuff's locked in the safe now. Mr Fitch found it. Thrilled to bits he is. Really thrilled – I've never seen him so excited. He's always so self-controlled.'

'Fitch! Excited? I'd like to have been here to see that.'

'He's gone to Budapest first thing this morning, won't be back in London till Tuesday, so he's locked it up till he's time to deal with it.'

Jimbo's mind raced. 'But you'll need to get in the safe between now and Tuesday, how are you going to manage? I was hoping my cheque would be here. End of month as we all know.'

'Fenella has the key!' She tapped the front of her silk shirt.

'Not down there?' Fenella nodded. 'The sacrifices you career girls make. I am filled with admiration. Have you seen the treasure?'

'I've to guard this key with my life. Mr Fitch has gone all mediaeval since we took this place over, if I lose it I shall be hung drawn and quartered. If you promise me not to tell, I'll open the safe for you, let you see it.'

'You've got to open it to give me my cheque, so . . . ' The telephone rang and he waited for her to answer it. When she'd finished speaking she said, 'I'll get one of the girls to take over and we'll go in the office and I'll let you take a peep.'

Fenella had the key on a chain hanging round her lovely slender neck. She bent down in front of the huge safe and, using the key and twiddling the knobs in a combination known only to a chosen few, unlocked it and swung back the door.

Jimbo felt privileged to handle the beautiful things Fenella brought out of the box. They'd all been carefully wrapped in tissue paper and it rustled invitingly as he removed it. But he didn't need enticing, the pieces were breathtakingly beautiful. There was no doubt, the silver belonged to the church. The chalice he was holding in his hand was dated 1655. Around the base were the words 'Thanks be to God'. The matching cup had the same date and the same words engraved. The big silver plates were engraved 'St Thomas à Becket 1739'. Fenella took out one of the candlesticks. It was engraved 'Sir Tristan Templeton 1821–1859'. The other one of the pair said 'Lady Mary Templeton 1824–1859'. His fingers traced the pattern winding round the stem of the candlestick and he noticed there were still traces of wax in the top and a drip of wax down one side. There was one magnificent candlestick which, as Pat had said, was tall enough when the three pieces were fitted together to stand on the floor.

'Why, Fenella, they're wonderful aren't they? Quite wonderful. They belong to the church, don't they?'

'Well, obviously they do.' She began to look upset and started hastily packing them away again in the safe. 'Better lock them up now.'

'Has he told the rector what he's found?' Jimbo said this knowing full well he hadn't.

Fenella locked the safe, replaced the chain round her neck and pushed the key down her shirt front.

'No. More than that I cannot say. Sorry. Going into the kitchens now are we, Mr Charter-Plackett?'

'Now look, I've known you two months now, it's about time you began to call me Jimbo. Please do. All my friends do. And thank you for showing me those things; it was a very precious moment for me. A real privilege.' He waved goodbye and went through the baize door and headed for the kitchens. But his mind wasn't on his work. Damn and blast. He had to act before Tuesday. That fool Fitch would probably send a chap down from a London auction house and the stuff would be spirited away and that would be that. In all conscience he couldn't let it happen. But who should he tell? How had the stuff got there in the first place? And why? Maybe Ralph would know. Yes, of course, Ralph would know. No one could hide those treasures in a house without the inhabitants knowing. All that banging and hammering putting the panelling up. Of course, he'd know all about it.

Jimbo left the Big House around twelve thirty, fully intending to call at the Store to check everything was in order and then go across to Ralph and Muriel's. As he was turning right out of the drive into Church Lane, Peter came past in his car. They both pulled up to hold a conversation through their open windows.

'Good day to you, Peter, had your Easter conference with Willie?'

'Jimbo, is there anything you *don't* know? Yes, I have. Everything OK with you? Good to see Harriet's looking fit and well.'

'Yes, she is, thanks. I say, in your perambulations around the paperwork in the rectory have you come across any details of gifts of altar silver to the church?'

Peter studied the question for a moment and decided no, he hadn't. 'Why?'

'There's some turned up at the Big House. They found it hidden behind some panelling yesterday. I've chatted up the receptionist and she's let me have a look. It's beautiful. Seventeenth, eighteenth and nineteenth century. Wonderful stuff. Can't stop now. I'll let you know more later today. What time will you be back?'

'Fourish.'

'OK then, see you around.'

He pulled up outside the Store. There was no escape. There was a queue for the post office and one at the till. Pat came in about a quarter to two. She took a chance by jumping the queue to hand him one of his own carrier bags.

'Eh! Pat, can't yer see there's a queue? Gone blind or something?'

'All right, all right, it's just a message.' She turned her back to everyone so they couldn't see the contents of the bag. Lowering her voice she said, 'Sneaked this out of the bin last night. It's some of the newspaper they were wrapped in. OK?'

Jimbo tapped the side of his nose with a forefinger and said, 'Thanks. Mum's the word. See you later when it's quieter.'

'Right.' Pat strolled past the queue, nose in the air, leaving them all wondering what was going on between her and Mr Charter-Plackett. They could wonder. Pat was determined that Mr Fitch plc wasn't getting away with this one. She might not go to church, well, except at Christmas, but there was a limit. You couldn't mess about with church stuff. Look at that time with Sharon MacDonald. Pinched them chalice things and next news she's knifed clean through from front to back. Dead as a dodo. So yours truly had to do something about it, or else. She shivered at the thought and trundled back to her cottage, wishing for the millionth time that she wasn't a widow with two kids to bring up. And what was worse, her Dad perhaps coming to live with her, now it looked as if he was losing his job with the council cuts.

Ralph wasn't at home when Jimbo called so he went next door to the rectory and rang the bell. What a difference Caroline and Peter had made since they came. Old Mr Furbank hadn't bothered at all, dust and cobwebs every-where.

The door opened. Caroline stood there, a twin on either hand.

'Jimbo! How nice. What a rare treat. Do come in. Say hello, you two.' The two of them hid their faces in her skirt and refused to speak.

'Alex! Beth! say hello to your old Uncle Jimbo. No? Never mind then. Peter in yet?'

'Yes, he's in his study drinking tea, would you like a cup?'

'Yes, please, had no lunch today, been so busy.'

'Go in then, and I'll find a piece of Sylvia's gingerbread for you.'

'Lovely.'

While he drank his tea and ate the gingerbread Jimbo filled Peter in on the story. When he'd finished Peter said, 'Sell it? How could he? It's patently obvious from what you say he can see it belongs to the church.'

'Exactly. If anyone should sell it, it should be the church. I say, wouldn't it help the old finances if we sold it? Just imagine what we could do with the money. This is a piece of the newspaper it was wrapped in.'

Peter took it from him and gently opened it out, smoothing the crumpled paper and laying it on his desk.

'June 1940. 1940. Yes, of course. Do you know what? I think they hid it up there because of the threat of invasion. Dunkirk, the Germans just across the Channel, all that valuable silver, to say nothing of the value to the villagers. Yes, I bet that's what happened. So Ralph's father would know about it, and whoever was rector at the time. And the joiner or the estate worker they used to fix the panelling. Quite a skilful job if it's never been noticed for the last fifty or more years.'

'Thing is, there's no one around now who could possibly remember.'

'Except Ralph. He'd only be a little boy. Let's ask him though.'

'Not at home today. I tried him first. We've got till Tuesday anyway. Till Fitch gets back.'

'You say it's beautiful?'

'Oh yes, in brilliant condition. We've got to get it back to the church, Peter. Even if we decide it's too valuable to have on the premises and decide to sell some of it, at least we could use the money for something specific and say we bought this and this with it. But I would dearly love for us to keep it and bring it out on high days and holy days. That would be bliss. It would have to be secured in some way, otherwise the insurance companies wouldn't touch it with a bargepole. I wouldn't like to be in Fitch's shoes if he sells it. You know what this village is like. He'd probably find his body cut into little pieces and burnt, and his head stuck on a pole and paraded round the village.' Jimbo shuddered at the thought. 'We'll see Ralph during the weekend, and then I'll ring on Tuesday and ask my tame receptionist when he's coming down again.'

'Should we all go together, do you think?'

'Well, I found out, Ralph used to own the house and his father certainly did when the stuff was hidden there, and you have a very definite vested interest. So, yes, we'll all go.'

Although it wasn't his day for being early Jimbo made sure he was in the Store the following morning to take the opportunity of having a word with Willie about the silver.

He came at his usual time.

'Morning Willie, come to collect your paper?'

'Yes.' Willie went to the shelf where the papers were displayed and selected the one he wanted.

Jimbo said. 'Willie, have you heard any rumours about old silver being found which belongs to the church?'

Willie's head came up from looking at his handful of change. 'Silver? Silver? What silver?'

Jimbo explained quietly, to one side so any customers coming in wouldn't overhear.

'Well, now, June 1940. Let me see.' He scratched his head and looked into the middle distance as he pondered the problem. 'Well, now, in June 1940 my old Dad was the verger. Yes, that's right. My Dad.'

Jimbo looked eagerly at him. 'He isn't still alive, is he?'

'No, no he died in 1943. Pneumonia got 'im when he was forty-four. Would garden in the pouring rain, he would. The rector then would be let me see, Reverend Edgar Levett, that's right, Reverend Edgar Levett. He's dead though. Went to London to 'is sister's funeral and got killed with a flying bomb. Ralph's father's died, of course, in Malaya, so there's no one left. They'd keep it very secret anyway, wouldn't they? Wouldn't be the sort of thing you'd tell in The Royal Oak of a night. Perhaps they were the only three who knew where it was. Silver you say, and you've seen it.'

'That's right. Beautiful stuff, Willie. We can't let the old fox get away with this.'

'Get away with it? It's as plain as the nose on your face, he'd be stealing it. He'd be a thief. That'd look good in the papers. "Company chairman steals parish silver". My paper would be rare and glad to get hold of a tale like that.'

'True. True. Mum's the word, Willie, don't tell a soul. The rector knows, and I know, and now you. Well, Pat does, because she's the one who found out.'

'Pat does? Hell's bells. All t'village 'll know by teatime. Well, the rector 'ad better do something about it and quick, or that Craddock Fitch'll need to flee for his life. You'll have a job on keeping it secret if Pat Duckett knows.'

'Willie! She's promised me faithfully she won't breathe a word.'

'Oh yes? I'll be off. I've a grave to dig, and a dozen and one things to attend to before my Sylvia and me get off on our 'olidays.'

Jimbo watched him leave. Everyone dead. What a blow. Still it was more than fifty years ago, it was only to be expected. He amused himself by imagining the newspaper headlines if it got out. Fitch plc would certainly be hopping about. Jimbo grinned. Then he remembered about his catering contract at the Big House and the money it was bringing in each month.

But it was to be more than two weeks before he needed to resolve that dilemma, for Craddock Fitch went from Budapest to Moscow and then on to Helsinki before returning home.

Chapter 3

Pat Duckett wandered early into The Royal Oak, hoping Willie and Sylvia would be in tonight. They'd be back from their holidays now, full of news. All week it had been quiet with only Jimmy and Vera to talk to. Might be a bit more lively if they came in. She pushed her way through the crowd hoping their favourite table might be free. It was. Pat took her port and lemon over and sat down on the settle. She surveyed the crowd. The bar was really buzzing tonight and not half. There were plenty of the real villagers in, but also a lot who'd come out from Culworth and around to enjoy the country atmosphere and the good beer Bryn stocked now. Not that Pat drank it. Rotten stuff. The downfall of her Duggie and not half.

Pat was determined not to mention about the silver being found up at the Big House. It would try her self-control and no mistake, but with her job with Jimbo at stake if she let on, she'd an awful lot to lose just for the sake of five minutes in the limelight. If she could prove to him she was irreplaceable with this bit of income on the side, ten pound notes in her hand and no questions asked, she might just start to have a bit better life. The kids cost so much to feed and clothe nowadays. And what with Dean doing so well at school he wouldn't want to be leaving at sixteen. Duggie would have been so proud. She watched the door hoping someone she knew would come in. Tonight it didn't matter who it was, she just needed to talk.

The swing doors suddenly burst open. It was Jimmy Glover waving a newspaper in the air.

'I've won! I've come up! After all these years, I've made it. I 'ave. I 'ave yer know, I've made it!' Jimmy shouted at the top of his voice.

Bryn came out from behind the bar. 'Jimmy you never have! You've never won the pools!'

'I 'ave, it's 'ere in black and white. I've just checked mi pools and I'm right, I've won.'

'How much?'

'Don't know. I don't know. But I've won and I'm pretty sure it's a lot of money. Twenty-five years I've been filling in the pools and tonight I've made it. At last! At last!'

Excitedly Pat stood up. She experienced a momentary shaft of jealousy. Why couldn't it be she who'd won? Not much chance of that seeing as she'd never got the hang of filling in pools coupons. She hastened across to congratulate him. 'Wonderful. Wonderful. I'm that pleased for yer, Jimmy, that pleased yer've no idea. What a turn up for the book. How much d'yer think yer've got then?'

'Dunno, but it'll be a lot. What will yer 'ave Pat?'

'Gin and tonic, seeing as you're paying. Aren't you lucky Jimmy? I can't believe it. Brilliant! Absolutely brilliant!'

Bryn shouted for his wife. 'Georgie! come out here, come on, come out here. Alan, get Jimmy a drink on the house in honour of his win. It could be thousands, Jimmy, thousands.'

'It could be a million but it won't, thousands 'll do for

me. Where's that Willie Biggs? 'As 'e come in yet? He's been telling me all these years I couldn't 'ope to win but I 'ave, I 'ave.'

'He'll be in soon, saw him come back from his holidays a couple of hours ago.' Bryn slapped Jimmy on the back and the customers gathered round to add their congratulations.

'By Jove, Jimmy yer'll be able to buy a new cap.'

'You'll have plenty of friends now Jimmy, and not half.'

'Congratulations Jimmy.'

'There'll be no speaking to you now, we shall 'ave to touch our forelocks to yer.'

'Some 'ope, I can remember Jimmy with the seat of his trousers 'anging out and Miss Evans lending him a spare pair she kept for when anyone wet 'emselves.'

'Aw shut up.'

Jimmy, quite beside himself with the thrill of his win, told Bryn it was drinks on him for everyone and he'd pay when he got his winnings.

'That new ale for me Alan, and don't be mean with it.'

'Gin and orange here, and a Cinzano and lemonade for my old girl.'

'You've a cheek, I'll give yer "old girl".'

'Ale for me, Alan, and be sharp about it, I've a thirst on me like I don't know what!'

Alan Crimble the barman, with his habitual ingratiating smile on his face, attended to their requests. Georgie, petite and pretty, added her congratulations to Bryn's.

'Wonderful for you Jimmy, I'm really pleased. Take care of it though, however much it is it'll soon disappear. Have you any plans?'

'I've thought about tonight many a time and I decided years ago that when it 'appened I'd set miself up in business.'

The whole bar erupted with laughter. 'You, set yerself up in business! That's a right laugh. What as?'

'A scrap-metal merchant?'

'A rag and bone man?'

'How about a gamekeeper? He'd be good at that. Plenty of experience!'

'No. I bet he's going to be a merchant banker.'

'By gum, the City 'ad better watch out. Jimmy'll 'ave 'em by the scruff inside a week.'

'International banking scandal, that'll be it.'

'No, no, "Unknown pools winner takes City by storm".'

Jimmy began to look hurt, and Georgie took it upon herself to stop the ribbing. 'That'll do. You lot watch out, Jimmy'll be showing you all the way to go home before long, won't you Jimmy?'

Jimmy tapped the side of his nose with his forefinger and grinned at her. 'They can laugh but I'll 'ave the last laugh.' He leant over the bar counter and whispered in Georgie's ear. She listened intently and the customers who'd been pulling his leg strained to hear.

'What a good idea that is.' Georgie winked at him and then said, 'You lot wait and see. You're all in for a surprise. When will you know how much you've won, Jimmy?'

'Monday or Tuesday, but I'll know for definite on Wednesday how much it is, that's when they declare the dividend. Perhaps they'll be arriving in a big Rolls Royce to let me know. I can't wait. Just fancy, the first Glover to be in the money! I shall celebrate by 'aving half a pint of cream delivered with the milk tomorrow, that Malcolm'll 'ave a shock and not half.'

'Might be an idea if yer paid yer bill, he told me last week he'd soon be stopping calling.'

'Don't worry, he'll be paid good and proper when I get mi 'ands on mi money.' Glass in hand, Jimmy went to his favourite spot opposite the settle nearest to the door and sat down with his newspaper to relive his excitement.

The other customers collected their free drinks from the bar and returned to their seats to mull over the unfairness of a ne'er-do-well coming into money when they'd spent all their lives working hard to earn a pittance. But Jimmy Glover didn't care. His day had come. Excitement got the better of him and he called out, 'I'll have a bag o' them salted nuts please, Bryn, if yer don't mind.'

Someone shouted: 'Oh, the last of the big spenders, is Jimmy.'

He remembered a saying of Miss Evans at school, and it was about all he did remember, '*There is a tide in the affairs of men, Which taken at the flood, leads on to fortune*'. He would do just that. He looked impatiently at the door, wanting Willie to come through it so he could tell him of his good fortune.

Jimmy sat relishing his time in the limelight. He'd show 'em. At last a chance to succeed, a chance to pull himself out of the mud and sit out in the sun, where often it seemed as though everyone sat except him. When he'd got organised he'd get another dog. A little Jack Russell like Sykes. Wouldn't call it Sykes though, there'd never be another Sykes. A lump came to his throat when he thought about his old friend. Eleven years of devotion, that dog had given him. Ah well. The emotion of the evening turned into a moroseness he found hard to dispel. As customers left they came across to thank him and congratulate him again, but he couldn't quite raise himself above his melancholy. If only his Mary had lived, he could have made her life so comfortable. All he had left of Mary was a few faded photos and her wedding ring in that carved wooden box of his mother's where he kept a lock of their baby's hair. And who had he to share his money with, now it had come? Nobody.

Pat went back to her favourite settle and sat opposite Jimmy.

'What *are* yer going to do with yer money then, Jimmy?'

'Don't know yet, Pat.'

'First thing yer can do is buy a new cap.'

Jimmy ignored her remark. 'I'll see how much it is first and then decide. I'd like to do mi cottage up. Put a bathroom in and 'ave a new kitchen. Get it painted and that, and then I'll set miself up in business.'

'What kind of business though?'

'Not telling.'

'That's mean. Not telling! What are you qualified to do then?'

'Nothing much. Look out, 'ere's Willie! Over 'ere Willie, a drink for Mr Biggs, Alan, if you please.' Willie bustled across and held out his hand. 'Let me shake hands with you Jimmy, Thelma knocked and she told me yer good news. First chap I've known who's won on the pools, after all I've said too. Congratulations, I'm really pleased and my Sylvia sends her love and says she's thrilled for yer. By Jove, eh Pat, it'll be a pound to speak to him now.'

Jimmy grunted. 'It will not. Like all these big winners say "it won't make any difference to me, I shall turn up for work on Monday as usual".'

'What work?' Pat and Willie began laughing, but stopped when they realised Jimmy was offended.

'You'll be able to go on holiday now, you'll be able to afford one of them glamorous cruises to the Caribbean on the QE2,' Willie said as he nodded his head in acknowledgement of Alan bringing his drink across to the table.

'Never mind about me going on holiday, you've just

come back from yours. How was Cornwall?'

'Well, I have to admit my wife and I had a lovely time, the weather was excellent, the sun shone most days and . . .' Pat and Jimmy looked at him as though they were in shock; Jimmy almost choked on his beer and Pat's mouth dropped open. 'We were able to go out every day. It's a lovely place is Cornwall for a honeymoon, have you ever been?' He looked innocently up at them, then took a long draught of his beer whilst he waited for their reactions.

'Willie!' Pat shouted. 'You 'aven't gone and got married without telling anyone, 'ave you?'

Jimmy looked incredulous. 'Married? You never 'ave, Willie, 'ave yer?'

Silence fell in the bar. All eyes were on Willie. He looked down at his drink, his face glowing with pleasure.

'Yes, as a matter of fact we 'ave.'

The other customers gathered round to hear the news.

'Where?'

'Here in the church.'

'Here in the church? Well, I never! When?'

'Day we left.'

Pat protested unbelievingly. 'But you left at half past nine, I saw the taxi come.'

'The rector married us at eight and we left at half past nine.' The customers offered their good wishes to Willie and his bride. 'Thank you very much indeed, I'll tell Sylvia when I get back, she'll be delighted.'

Pat registered her disappointment. 'We never 'eard nothing about banns being read.'

'Special licence.'

'Oh right. Crafty that was, crafty. Well, I'm right surprised at you, Willie. Verger at the church and sneaking in to get married and saying nothing to nobody. We'd have liked to give you a big send-off. I'm really disappointed.'

'Well, that was just it. Sylvia wanted a quiet wedding.'

'It was certainly that and no mistake.'

'Our wedding service was very important to us Pat, and we wanted to be able to concentrate on what we were saying, so that was what we decided to do. Rector and Dr Harris were a bit disappointed, but they agreed with us in the end.'

'Who else was there? 'Cos whoever it was, they've kept mum and no mistake.'

'The rector of course, Dr Harris with the twins, Sir Ralph and Muriel.'

'Oh I see, they could be there but we couldn't who've known you all these years. I'm right offended Willie and no mistake.'

Jimmy grunted, 'A chap 'as a right to get married 'ow he likes. At least he's made an honest woman of 'er.'

Willie objected. 'That's enough, thank you. What's between Sylvia and me is entirely private.'

Pat laughed. 'All right, Willie, keep yer hair on.' She turned to Jimmy and asked, 'Will you be next then, now you've got all this money?'

Jimmy brushed his moustache with the back of his forefinger and smiled wryly. 'Well, I 'ad thought of popping the question to you, but maybe it wouldn't be a good idea.'

Pat was enraged at the thought and told him so in no uncertain terms. 'Married to you? Not Pygmalion likely. I've enough on my plate without adding you and yer smelly clothes and yer ferrets and geese to mi troubles. If I marry it'll be to money.'

'But that's just what he's got, Pat, now. Money.' Willie grinned at her and for a moment she hesitated, and then said, 'He'd have to be a millionaire before I'd marry 'im.'

'Well, he might be, yer never know.'

Jimmy offered his congratulations to Willie and said he was right pleased for him and he hoped they'd be very happy.

The conversation in the bar was rising to a crescendo, the news of Jimmy's win and now Willie's marriage causing consternation. 'We don't get far but we do see life,' they were saying. It was nearly as good as that night when poor Sharon McDonald, God rest her soul, and her mother had that fight here in the bar, or that day when the bar was packed and Betty McDonald thumped Willie on the nose and came close to punching the rector. A few left earlier than they had intended so they could spread the news. Others stayed on in the hope that even more news might be revealed before the evening was over, and better still, more free drink.

Jimmy interrupted a story of Pat's about the school and said, 'I've been thinking that now Bryn's dining room has been open a whole week and they'll have got into the swing of things, would you like to join me for a meal tonight?'

'Well, Jimmy, that would be lovely.' Pat said not admitting that she had already eaten at home, but it had only been beefburgers and chips with ice cream to finish. She couldn't bear the thought of missing a free meal. It was the first time Jimmy had ever offered anything of the kind.

'What about you, Willie, do you fancy going and collecting your Sylvia and joining us? We could 'ave a joint celebration as yer might say. You owe it to us for us 'aving missed yer wedding. I'm paying. Bryn'll see me all right till next week.'

'Well, thank you very much.' Willie stood up. 'I'll go get her right now.'

As he walked home up Stocks Row, Willie added up how many days he'd been married. Nine days, nine whole days. How on earth they'd managed to keep it secret he would never know. He chuckled to himself when he recollected how Mr Harris had leapt about from the organ to the altar steps and back. Good job he could play the organ as well as be rector! Lovely music it was, he couldn't half play. When he saw his Sylvia coming down the aisle he couldn't believe how lovely she'd looked. Dressed in a kind of silvery grey she was, which just matched her lovely big grey eyes. She'd put her hand in his with such love in her eyes he felt very humble. Then of course Sir Ralph couldn't find the ring and searched every pocket till it finally came to light in Muriel's handbag. Her face was scarlet and no mistake. They'd all laughed. That was the best thing about a quiet wedding it was so much more, what was the word, friendly, yes that was it, more personal like. The rector had played some lovely triumphant music when they'd walked down the aisle, stopping as they reached the door so that the village wouldn't hear and wonder what was going on. Then they'd had a lovely champagne breakfast in the rectory and hey presto, the taxi was there and they were off. Not many men in his position had a baronet as his best man.

They'd posed for photos in the church itself. Dr Harris had taken them, and now they were home and he'd seen them he knew it really had happened.

'Sylvia, where are you love?'

'In here, have you seen Jimmy?' Willie found her in their little kitchen just beginning to make their evening meal.

'Yes, he's thrilled to bits, he wants to know if we'd like to go over there for a meal in Bryn's new dining room to celebrate with him.'

'That would be lovely. Right now? Tonight you mean?'

'Yes. They all know, love, about us.' He stood behind her and linked his hands around her waist.

'How did they find out?'

'I told 'em.' Willie kissed her ear.

'Willie!'

'Why not? I'm that proud of yer. They're all gobsmacked and not half. All the village will know by morning.'

'And why not? Shall I get changed?'

'No, yer lovely as you are. Come on, love, I'm starving. We can take the wedding photos round to Ralph and Muriel on Monday, I'll be too busy tomorrow with it being Sunday. Come on then, put that down. Let's be off.'

Chapter 4

Sir Ralph was just finishing his breakfast and enjoying the whole experience of being looked after by his adoring wife when they heard the postman at the door. Muriel never could resist seeing what he had brought the moment it came, so she'd left the breakfast table to pick it up from the mat. Pericles, his black nose shining bright against his white coat, yapped as vigorously as his age permitted, and stood on the letters. Muriel pushed him off and as she bent down, there came loud, urgent banging on the front door. It made Muriel jump. She opened the door to find Willie Biggs standing there.

'Oh it's you, Willie, you made me jump. Good morning, how are you?'

'Very well, thank you, and you?'

'Very well, thank you.'

'I know I'm early but I've a lot on this morning with being away. I've brought our wedding photos. Sylvia and I would like you to choose what you want and let me know and then we'll have them done as a gift to you and Ralph.'

'There's no need . . .'

'Absolutely, I insist. It's not every day a man gets married.'

'No, that's right. Well, thank you, thank you very much. I'm really looking forward to seeing them. Goodbye Willie.'

'Good morning.' He stepped briskly away. Muriel returned to the dining room.

'Look, Ralph dear, the wedding photos. I can't wait to look. Let's clear a space, we mustn't get them messy.' Muriel smiled at Ralph and his heart turned over. He never quite got over the delight of being with her again after all their years apart. Coming back to the village and finding her and persuading her to marry him had been the best day's work he'd ever done. He smiled back and then moved his plate to make room. Caroline's photographs had come out excellently and they were delighted with them.

'Oh! Look at this one, Ralph, you do look serious.'

'It's a serious business giving away a bride, and being best man too. This one of you is good, very good indeed. We must have that one. Look at this one, Willie's grinning like a cat that's been at the cream! That one of Sylvia and me is good.'

'Let's have another look later on and decide which we want. We mustn't ask for too many, they're not that well off. You've a lot of post this morning, Ralph. Shall I put it in your study?'

'Yes, please, my dear. I've nearly finished. Is there another slice of toast?'

'Of course, as many as you like.'

Muriel took Ralph's extra slice in to him and as she handed it to him she kissed the top of his head. She stroked his white hair, kissed him again and said, 'Your hair needs cutting.'

'Yes. I know, that's on my agenda for this week. In fact, I think I'll go up to town to get it cut.'

'Up to town? Don't you mean Culworth?'

'No. Town. Come with me and we'll go to the theatre, or the opera if you prefer, and you can do some shopping. I have a few business matters I need to attend to, so you could shop while I . . . '

'Ralph! I'd love that, except I shall go sightseeing instead of shopping. Yes, definitely I'll come. Have you finished, dear?'

'Yes, thank you. That marmalade is excellent, you must compliment Jimbo on it the next time you go in the Store. Tomorrow it is then. Look in *The Times* and choose a couple of theatres and we'll leave tomorrow morning first thing. I'm sure Ron and Sheila will have Pericles for you at short notice. I'll open my post while you do that.'

'I'll clear the table first and tidy the kitchen and then I'll look.' Muriel busied herself clearing away and putting her kitchen to rights. Moving to this bigger house had been a wrench at first but now she wondered how she had ever managed in such a small house as Glebe Cottage. London, how she loved it. They'd been to the South of France and Ralph was planning for them to go to New York later in the year, and she'd seen masses of places in Australia when they'd had their honeymoon there, but London she loved best of all. Her heritage she called it, and Ralph always smiled when she said that.

Muriel was putting the bread knife in the dishwasher and giving her kitchen a final inspection before switching it on, when Ralph shouted: 'MURIEL!!!' She jumped so much she dropped the bread knife and it crashed to the floor. She clutched her heart and said, 'Oh, Ralph, whatever is it?' She rushed into the study expecting to find him taken ill.

Ralph was sitting at his desk holding a letter in his hand, his face, his handsome face, red with excitement. As soon as he caught sight of her he said, 'Had you heard that the Methodist chapel is closing?'

'Closing? No, is it?'

'Well apparently, yes. They are closing this one and building a large extension to their church in Little Derehams. They've always been a funny lot in Little Derehams.'

'Ralph! Really.'

'Well, you know what I mean.'

'Why should the Methodist chapel closing be so important to you? You've never attended there.'

'No, my dear, I haven't. This letter is from the council telling me all about it.'

Muriel sat down on a chair and decided to await Ralph's explanation. He turned over the page and continued reading. Muriel sat admiring him while he did so. In fact she never tired of admiring him, and to think that at one time, to her shame, she didn't fancy the idea of his lovely aristocratic profile being beside her on the pillow each morning. What a foolish, misguided person she'd been. The Methodist chapel closing. Well. It had been there, on the spare land, for something like one hundred and forty years.

Ralph put down the letter and said, 'The spare land, as everyone calls it, belonged to my family. It was my great-great-grandfather who gave permission for the Methodists to build their chapel, on a kind of token rent basis. One florin each New Year's Day, it was. I remember them coming up to the Big House to pay my father for it. I always understood that my mother sold the entire estate to the council after my father was killed, including that piece called the spare land. But they can't find the deeds for it in the archives and have discovered that though the council *assumed* they'd bought the spare land at the time they bought the estate, they now find that the land was never legally transferred to them. So-o-o, I still own all the land surrounding Turnham Beck, would you believe. What I need to do is to find the deeds for it.'

'But what use is it to you, Ralph? It's all rough scrub land. Though the trees are beautiful, I always love the beeches in the spring, their leaves look so fresh and most especially green then, and the willows with their twigs dabbling in the beck, and I do look forward to the ducklings in the spring.'

'Use to me? If it is proved that the council have never in fact owned it and it has been mine all these years without me knowing it, then I shall be able to do what I've always wanted to do and provide houses for village people to rent.'

Muriel jumped up, horrified. 'Houses on it? Oh Ralph, how could you?'

'But don't you want villagers to be able to stay in the village? Young married people can't afford to buy the houses now. If they could rent they would stay, if not the village will die.'

'But the beech trees Ralph, they'll all be chopped down. And the lovely beck! Pericles loves sniffing about down there and paddling in the water. It would be dreadful to destroy it. Quite dreadful.' As though on cue Pericles came trotting in to the study, reminding Muriel it was time for his walk. She bent down to pat him.

'Muriel, my dear, just because I am proposing to build houses it doesn't mean I shall get rid of the beck, where on earth would all the water go if I did? No, it would be incorporated in the design, and you'd still be able to walk Pericles there because it's a public footpath right from ancient times and would have to be preserved.'

'Are you sure?'

'Yes, I am.' Ralph firmly nodded his head and then said, 'Anyway it isn't definite yet. When you come back we'll go in the attic and get down that old trunk from the Big House and go through the papers in there to see if we can find anything to throw light on the matter.' He stood up, took her hand, raised it to his lips and kissed it. 'Don't let yourself become distressed my dear, and don't tell anyone of our conversation this morning. Not a word.' Ralph pressed a finger to her lips and smiled. Muriel smiled faintly at him and then retreated to find her coat and gloves and Pericles' lead.

Apart from their disagreement about Jimmy and him snaring rabbits, Muriel decided this was the biggest conflict they had had to face since they got married. As she unclipped Pericles' lead and watched him scamper off, how did he manage at his age, she paused to enjoy the trees and the sound of the beck running along. Houses here on this lovely piece of land. Even though spring had not yet come, with all the rain they'd had, the grass and the trees were looking quite fresh, and just here and there were the first signs of new life rising in the trees; tiny buds coming on the twigs and the grass looking perkier after the long winter. She stood on the little footbridge which the council had constructed over the beck and leant on the rail to watch the water dashing over the pebbles. Pericles leapt in and paddled under the bridge. She called to him and as he appeared from underneath he looked up and wagged his tail. She tried to imagine houses, houses, houses. Fences and garages, lawns and herbacious borders, bicycles abandoned on the footpaths, children's slides peering over the tops of the fences . . . Oh no, Ralph, it simply wouldn't do.

When she and Pericles got home Ralph was not downstairs. She called his name but got no response. Then she heard loud thuddings coming from the attic, where she found Ralph already struggling with the trunk.

'You're back, my dear. Shall we get the trunk down the stairs or shall we look at the papers up here?'

'Ralph, I don't want you to build houses on that land.'

He looked at her with surprise. 'Look at it another way, Muriel. Already three of the village cottages are in the hands of weekenders. In addition your cottage is sold to someone who is only here from time to time. Toria Clark's old cottage is going the same way because Dickie and Bel Tutt are never here. Let's suppose some young couple from the village want to live here and bring up their family. Where would they live? Nowhere. And that means that the school numbers will slowly get so small it won't be worth keeping it open. Then there will be an even bigger decline because we shan't be able to attract people to live here if they have a family. They won't want to be bussing their little children into Culworth every day, will they? Jimbo's store would suffer, the church would suffer and The Royal Oak would suffer . . .'

Muriel couldn't help smiling. 'That mightn't be a bad thing after Saturday night's rumpus!'

Ralph laughed. They still hadn't got over watching half the village doing a conga round the green after closing time, led by Jimmy who must have had the hangover of all time the following morning. 'Still, he did have something to celebrate, didn't he?'

'Yes, he did. I do see your point, Ralph, about the school. Michael Palmer was talking to me about it only the other day, he said if there were any more cuts in education, closing the school will be one of their next economies. Let's take the trunk downstairs and have a coffee in front of the fire and look through the papers. It could take us all day, but never mind, we've nothing else on our agenda today.'

They had both coffee and lunch sitting by the fire sorting out the trunk. Ralph kept getting waylaid by reading the papers and reminiscing about the old life. He even found some old estate account books in which Muriel's father's name as head gardener appeared. 'Look, Muriel, Henry Hipkin £4. Again here the following week, Henry Hipkin £4. That was before you were born. He was quite well paid for those times, wasn't he? Because he'd have the house and all the fruit and vegetables he could eat. Possibly they'd even provide him with meat when they slaughtered a pig or a sheep.' Muriel despite her reluctance about the whole project became quite excited, and delved into the trunk with delighted cries when she found something of interest. Then, as she went to take their lunch tray into the kitchen, Ralph gave a triumphant shout. 'Here we are, I've found the deeds.' To Muriel it sounded like a death knell.

When they set off the next morning for London Ralph had the deeds in his briefcase, along with the letters which had been exchanged when the estate was sold.

That morning Linda arrived at the Store buzzing with news. Last minute as usual, she was hurriedly unlocking the post office grille and setting herself up for business and at the same time telling Jimbo what her cousin Kev had said.

'So-o-o our Kev knows all about it because he works in the planning department, you see. That'll be one twenty-five, Mrs Goddard. Lovely day isn't it? Thank you. Next! Twenty-five pence first class, right thank you. Where was I? Oh yes, so he says that the spare land where the Methodist chapel is or was as you might say because they're leaving, did you know? Anyway they are, and I shouldn't be telling you this but I can't keep it to myself, he says the spare land all these years has belonged to Sir Ralph and not to the council. And there they've been building the footbridge, putting the wastebins there, cutting the trees down when all the time it wasn't theirs in the first place, and letting it to the fair each Stocks Day and keeping the rent. I bet Sir Ralph could claim all that money back. Nice little packet for him and no mistake, don't you think Mr Charter-Plackett?'

'I don't think the rent from the fair would amount to enough for Sir Ralph to make a fuss about. Linda, can it keep, if it's top secret this isn't the place to be discussing it, is it?'

'Sorry Mr Charter-Plackett, I'll tell you the rest in my coffee break.'

Jimbo didn't have to wait until Linda's coffee break, because the very next customer who came in launched herself into the latest piece of gossip.

'Have you heard, Mr Charter-Plackett, that the council's building a hundred houses on the spare land when the chapel goes? Doesn't seem right, does it?'

'A hundred houses? They couldn't surely, it isn't big enough.'

'Well, that's what the council's going to do. Scandalous isn't it? Downright scandalous. I bet Sir Ralph won't like that at all. He'll want to keep the village like it's always been. We'll have to get a campaign up. It'll carry some weight though with a titled person leading it.'

'Where did you learn this?'

'From my niece, she works in the council offices doing the tea trolley. She hears everything that goes on there, believe me. And there's certainly plenty going on. The management there 'as wild parties, you'd be surprised at what they get up to. Oh, yes! Disgusting! They do say' – Jimbo's customer leant closer and whispered in his ear – 'they do wife swapping at their parties!'

Jimbo got a piece of paper and a pen from behind the till and said, 'Give me the telephone number and I'll see if Harriet and I can get invited.'

For a moment the customer took him seriously and then realised his eyes were twinkling. 'Oh, Mr Charter-Plackett, you nearly caught me there. Anyway I'll keep you informed.' She winked at him, picked up her groceries and left.

Jimbo contemplated the idea of one hundred houses and what it would do to his turnover. Magnificent. A completely magnificent idea. Still, if the land belonged to Ralph like Linda said it did, there wouldn't be a hope in hell of houses being built on it. Someone had got their wires crossed. Still, a hundred houses. With all those new customers the Store would thrive, with his outsider catering flourishing like it always did, the mail-order business coming along nicely under his mother-in-law's eagle eye and with the contract for the catering at the Big House already in the bag, they'd really be in the money. Jimbo rubbed his hands together at the prospect.

'And why is the proprietor of the Turnham Malpas Village Store rubbing his hands with such glee?'

Jimbo swung round and saw Harriet. 'Darling! Where did you spring from?'

'The mail-order office, mother needed an extra pair of hands so I've been helping in there.'

'I did say you musn't, not in your condition as they say.'

'I'm as fit as a flea, Jimbo, and with three months to go I've still got some energy to spare.'

43

'Don't overdo it, darling, please.'

'I won't. So why were you rubbing your hands?'

Jimbo took her arm and led her into the store room. With Harriet seated on his stool, he told her the morning's gossip. 'So we shan't say a word. I don't care who the hell builds the houses, but they will mean a big increase in business for us.'

'It will take years, absolutely years, to get them built. By the time they've had protests and inquiries and things we could be looking at three or four years before anyone even puts a spade in.'

'I rather think they'll need more than a spade to dig the foundations for a hundred houses.'

'We'll see, we'll see. Ralph and Muriel will be opposed so we shall have to tread carefully.'

'Exactly. We shan't come down on either side, we shall remain aloof from the hurly-burly.'

'Some hope, some hope.'

Chapter 5

The following Saturday night Willie and his Sylvia went by arrangement to have a drink in The Royal Oak with Pat and Jimmy, Pat's neighbour Vera, and Vera's husband Don. They would have infinitely preferred to have stayed at home and watched a video they'd borrowed from Jimbo's newly installed video lending library, but Jimmy had been insistent.

'Vera and Don were away last week at that funeral so they didn't 'ave a chance to have a drink to celebrate you getting wed and me winning the pools. So you'll 'ave to come, yer both getting into right homebirds and it won't do.'

'All right, all right,' Willie reluctantly agreed. 'Seven o'clock sharp then.'

'Well, that's good and dress up a bit and I'll take you for another meal in Bryn's dining room, I'm getting a right liking for it. So don't eat before yer come out.'

Willie passed the message on to his Sylvia and they both made a special effort to look smart. About five minutes to seven they entered the bar. There were scarcely any customers and their host held centre stage. Sylvia gasped when she saw Jimmy standing at the bar. It was his feet she noticed first – instead of his old calf-high, well worn dirty boots, he was wearing brand new black shoes. He stood with one well-shod foot resting on the brass rail below the front of the bar, an elbow propped on the bar counter.

'Why Jimmy, you do look smart. Look at him, just look at him Willie.'

The transformation didn't stop at his feet. Gone was the foul old flat cap, gone the old green jacket and the innumerable jumpers he always wore. They had been replaced by a smart dark grey suit, white shirt and a dazzling tie. He was clean-shaven and his hair well barbered. His moustache, which had been a village institution from time immemorial, had gone too; the newly shaved top lip looked pale in contrast to his narrow well tanned face.

Willie nudged his elbow. 'I can't believe the change, Jimmy, you're almost unrecognisable.'

'Shows what money can do!'

Sylvia felt the quality of the material the suit was made of. 'It certainly does. You look a right catch and not half.'

'Thanks, Sylvia thanks. I'm glad yer like me like this. Never had money to spare before, yer see.'

'Well, go on,' Willie said. 'Tell us 'ow much yer've got.'

'Seeing as I've known you since we were in nappies, I'll tell yer, but I don't want them busybodies to know.' He nodded his head in the direction of the three other customers. 'Don't want 'em coming begging, yer see.' He mouthed rather than spoke the words. 'Fifty thousand one hundred pounds and seventy-five pence.'

Willie whistled in amazement. 'I don't believe it. I never thought you'd do it, yer know. It's nothing short of a miracle.'

'That's 'ow I see it. A miracle no less.' Sylvia reached up

and gave him a kiss. 'I'm really, really glad for you Jimmy. Make the best of it, don't fritter it away.'

Jimmy tapped the side of his long thin nose and said, 'I 'ave mi plans and not 'alf. Wait and see.'

Vera and Don Wright and Pat arrived to join the party. They chose a bigger table than usual and all sat down. Willie made a suggestion. 'Hadn't we better organise a table in the dining room? It might get full with it being Saturday.'

Jimmy assured him that he'd already taken care of that. Vera was pressing him to reveal how much he'd actually won when the door opened and in came the rector. Peter, his head bent because of his height, stood in the entrance looking at the occupants of the bar. He looked anxious and out of breath.

Willie put down his glass, wiped his mouth with the back of his hand and called out, 'Good evening, sir, are you looking for me?'

'Ah, there you are. Good evening everybody. Willie, I'm afraid we have an emergency on our hands. You'll have to come, there's been a break-in at the church hall.'

'Oh no! Have they taken much?'

'Well, I thought you'd know that better than me. Can you come right away? Sorry to break up the party.'

Don said, 'We'll all come, Rector, they might still be in there.'

'Right, thanks, that's a good idea.' The men stood up to go, and Pat and Vera with them. Willie suggested that the womenfolk shouldn't come, it wasn't safe, but Pat said, 'And miss all the fun? Not likely. Come on, Sylvia, bring yer umbrella, we might need it.'

The six of them hurried down Stocks Row, round into Church Lane, through the big double gates and up the drive to the church hall. It was in darkness. Willie went first and tried the main door. 'It's open!' He felt on the wall for the main switches and flooded the hall with light. It was completely empty.

A lone trumpet burst into 'Here comes the bride' and from nowhere came accompanying voices lustily singing the words. When the song was finished the doors from the kitchen and the small hall opened, and out into the main hall poured almost every friend and neighbour and child Willie knew. Sylvia blushed bright red with sheer delight. They all surged forward to shake their hands and wish them happiness.

'Weren't at the wedding so we had to celebrate somehow!'

'Bet that's surprised you, hasn't it?'

'It was all Dr Harris's idea, wasn't it, Rector?'

Peter laughed and nodded. 'Yes, you're right, it was.'

In the midst of the excitement Willie turned to Peter and said, 'Now, sir, that was a trick you played on us and not half. Hall broken into, what a tale!'

'It was true, it was true. All these people broke in, I had to come and tell you, didn't I?' Peter smiled at him, enjoying the joke.

'Is Dr Harris here?'

'She's at home with the twins, I'm going back shortly and she's going to come over to join you.'

Jimbo Charter-Plackett climbed on a chair. 'Ladies and gentlemen, before we go any further with tonight's proceedings, my daughter Flick has something to say. Come along, Flick, where are you?'

There was a moment's hesitation and then Flick appeared in the kitchen doorway, carrying a huge bouquet. Everyone smiled. They all loved Flick; they loved her happy personality, they loved her smile, they loved to hear her chatter. They awaited her speech.

She curtsied and then said, 'Mr and Mrs Biggs, these flowers are for you from all of us, to say how pleased we are that you have got married, and we all hope you will be very happy.' She whispered confidentially, 'And there's lots of presents in the small hall, you wouldn't believe how many!' She curtsied again and gave Sylvia the flowers. They all laughed and clapped and Sylvia bent down and gave her a hug and a kiss.

Jimbo climbed back up on the chair. 'Right, ladies and gentlemen, quiet please. Quiet please. Now's the time to let the bridal couple lead the way to the buffet. A right royal buffet we've laid on for a right royal pair. Forward march!'

They all held back while the bride and groom reached the front of the crowd and then followed them into the small hall. From end to end of the far wall was a table laden with food and in the centre of the table was a beautiful two-tier wedding cake, with a small silver vase of flowers decorating the top. The flowers were deep pink and around the edges of the cake were icing sugar-flowers in varying shades of pink complementing the real flowers on the top. Swirls of silvery white and pink ribbons decorated the table around the cake. On another table presents were piled high, awaiting presentation. Sylvia burst into tears of joy. Willie lent her his handkerchief, and then put his arm around her shoulders, his face alight with pleasure.

'Speech, speech,' the guests demanded.

'My Sylvia and I would like to thank you for this lovely party, it must be the best kept secret in Turnham Malpas for centuries, we'd absolutely no idea.' Someone at the back shouted. 'We'll go some to keep a secret better than you, Willie Biggs! Marrying without any of us knowing.' Everyone laughed. Willie acknowledged the quip and continued his speech. 'And as for you, Jimmy, you conniving old so-and-so, I'll see you later. Thank you again and again, we shan't forget all your kindness in planning this. We're both very happy, we hope you all will be too. Here's to a wonderful evening!'

After everyone had finished eating, and Willie and his Sylvia had cut the cake, Venetia Mayer, who had disappeared moments before, struggled in through the doorway with a gigantic box, wrapped in wedding gift paper. Everyone crowded round. What on earth could it possibly be? Trust Venetia to come up with something dramatic! Jeremy refused to tell. 'Wait and see,' he said, 'wait and see.'

Sylvia began tearing off the paper. She opened the lid and out floated three huge heart-shaped silver hydrogen-filled balloons. They all craned their necks to see what was written on them. One said 'Congratulations', the second one said 'Willie loves Sylvia' and the third 'Sylvia loves Willie'. Willie tied them by their ribbons to a chair and they all cried 'Give the bride a kiss'. So he did. Then Jimbo put on a tape and they began dancing. Willie and Sylvia started off the first dance all by themselves. Willie wasn't up to dancing, he hadn't done it since he used to go to the Palais in Culworth as a young man, but he made a brave show for his Sylvia's sake.

Caroline let herself into the rectory at eleven o'clock that night. She called upstairs, 'Peter, I'm making myself a cup of tea, would you like one?'

'Yes, please, darling. Had a good time?'

'Excellent, I'm exhausted! Won't be long. Twins OK?'

'Both fine, not a peep out of them all evening.'

Caroline took the tea upstairs and put it on Peter's side table. She looked in on the twins and tucked the blankets more closely around Beth, who had a habit of kicking off all her bedclothes and waking chilled to the bone in the middle of the night. Alex lay on his back, a hand either side of his head, sleeping deeply, his likeness to Peter increased as the weeks went by. There was no hiding the fact he was his. None at all.

Caroline got ready for bed and climbed in beside Peter, who was sitting up reading. He asked how she'd enjoyed the evening.

'Wonderful. I'm so glad the idea came to me. We couldn't let them get married so secretly and the village not have a chance to celebrate, could we? I have to admit to wondering if they would both cope, but they did. We've had a fantastic night. Jimbo's a brilliant master of ceremonies, he gets everyone going, however resistant they are. We've danced and sung and played games, but I suddenly went dreadfully tired so I've left them all to it. Jimbo has put Scottish dancing tapes on now and Alan Crimble, who says he's part Scottish, is teaching them the dances. They were all laughing so much I don't think they'll learn anything at all. What a night!'

'It was the most superbly kept secret, darling. Here's your tea.'

'Thanks, it was, wasn't it? I don't know how we managed it, knowing the propensity of this village for gossip! Whilst I was at the party I had a talk with Pat Duckett. I'm going to ask Jimbo if he can find some more work for her with his outside catering. She is very strapped for cash, she was telling me at the party how hard things are for her.'

'I thought you went to enjoy yourself, not be a rector's wife.'

'Can't help it, people will confide in me. I must have that kind of face.'

'Well, I love that kind of face. Jimbo, Ralph and I are going up to the Big House on Monday for our appointment with the renowned Craddock Fitch. I feel Jimbo is slightly less enthusiastic than he was, but Ralph is furious about the whole affair.'

'Did he know anything about them hiding the silver?'

'Nothing at all, he was away at prep school when it all happened. In any case they wouldn't tell a little boy, would they? It would have been too much to expect him to keep it secret. He's determined, however, to get it all back where it belongs, even if we decide to sell some of it to help with the repairs to the tower. I can see we could be in for some fireworks. I really don't see how Fitch can possibly lay claim to it at all. He must be off his trolley.'

'Perhaps power has gone to his head. That tea was lovely, I felt so dry.'

'Let me take your cup. Happy?'

'Oh yes, in paradise actually.' Caroline snuggled down under the duvet. Peter lay down beside her. He took hold of her hand and held it to his lips and kissed it.

'I'm glad. So am I. God bless. Goodnight.'

Chapter 6

Jeremy Mayer greeted them at the door when they arrived.

'Welcome to Turnham House, Rector.' He shook hands with Peter. 'And welcome to you, Sir Ralph, pleasure to see you. Hello, Jimbo, how goes it?' Jimbo observed that Jeremy had put on even more weight since his life had become secure. His podgy hand clasped Jimbo's in a damp grip and Jimbo unobtrusively returned his now clammy hand to his trouser pocket and rubbed his palm on his handkerchief.

'Good morning Jeremy,' Peter said. 'Long time no see.'

'Been busy, Rector, you know how it is, new project, new fields to conquer, all takes time. Would you like to come this way? Ah! Here's Venetia. Looking delightful as always.'

Venetia, looking very trim, was wearing a white plush tracksuit decorated with a purple yoke and a purple stripe down the legs of the trousers. Her excessively black hair was held away from her face by a white towelling band. Her tan, assisted by heavy makeup, was as deep as it could be. She greeted them as though they'd just returned from a hazardous expedition to some distant shore.

'How wonderful to see you, Peter!' She offered her cheek for a kiss. He bent his head and dutifully complied. Jimbo she greeted by flinging her arms around him and kissing him soundly on both cheeks. 'Jimbo! you darling. I must remember to visit the Store more often, I'd forgotten what a lovely man you are.' She turned to Ralph and coyly offered him her hand to shake. 'Sir Ralph, what a pleasure it must be for you to come back to your old home! You'll find it vastly changed. But much improved. So warm now with the new central heating! When you've finished your appointment, come and find me and I'll show you round, then you can see the improvements for yourself. Jeremy, my love, will you show everyone to Cra . . . Mr Fitch's office?'

'Just in the process, dear girl.' He waddled off in front of them towards what Ralph remembered as the library. To look at him no one would have guessed how deeply he was suffering. Standing in the hall he'd seen ghosts from his childhood. The butler crossing the hall with his father's post on the silver salver. His nanny holding his hand and walking with him to the front door to take him for his walk. His mother, smelling of lavender, pulling on her gloves waiting to go to church with Father. Himself as a small boy holding her hymn book, dressed in his best which he hated. His heart bled at Venetia's words. Improvements indeed! Desecration would be nearer the mark. He was damned if this interloper was getting away with selling the church silver, if indeed that was what it was. Vulgar upstart, coming into his home and throwing his weight about. Damned if he'd let it happen. As he entered the library he stiffened his spine and prepared to meet the enemy.

His enemy was a slightly-built man of medium height, pale of face, looking to be in his middle to late sixties. The fierce, belligerent expression in his intense blue eyes matched well with the slightly sneering smile on his lips. His thick bushy hair was silver-white, his skin the smooth texture of a much younger man. He rose to his feet as they entered.

Jeremy introduced them. Craddock Fitch shook hands with them in turn, giving them an effusive welcome which didn't quite reach his eyes. 'Mayer, find chairs for my guests, please.'

Jeremy pulled chairs out and made a half circle with them in front of Mr Fitch's desk, and then stood to one side. Mr Fitch inquired if they would like coffee. They all three refused.

'Well, then, Charter-Plackett?' Mr Fitch looked across the library and saw Jeremy standing by the window. 'I'll call you up if I need you, Mayer.' Crestfallen, Jeremy quietly left the room. Ralph gritted his teeth. Peter pondered on the reasons for Mr Fitch's aggressiveness.

'Yes?' Mr Fitch looked at each of them in turn.

Jimbo nodded to Ralph, who cleared his throat. 'It has been brought to our attention that in the course of your alterations to this house, you have found certain articles of silver which, upon inspection, have proved to belong to the village church.'

'Have I?'

Ralph said an emphatic 'Yes.'

'And if I have, what then?'

'They belong to the church not to the house. We have concluded they were brought here secretly during the Second World War when England was threatened with invasion, namely June 1940. Obviously the intention was to return them to the church when hostilities ceased. In fact all three of the men we assume were concerned, including my father, died before the end of the war, so no attempt was made to recover the silver, because no one else knew where they had hidden it. It should be returned forthwith.'

'On whose authority?'

'The authority of all right-minded persons.'

'I bought this house, lock, stock and barrel. The roof in need of repair is mine, the grounds in need of attention are mine, the walls, the stables, the garden, anything and everything in it is mine. I learned when I had it surveyed that there was dry rot in the east wing, but I didn't say that bit isn't mine, I took it all as it was. Therefore the silver is mine and mine alone. Good morning, gentlemen.' He rose to his feet, a slight smile at one corner of his mouth. His eyes flicked from one to the other, assessing their reaction, but not really caring.

Peter quietly requested an opportunity to see what had been found.

'In deference to your clerical collar, yes, certainly you may. Best take your chance, I'm taking it up to town in the next few days, you won't be able to see it again. Charter-Plackett, I need a word. Do you wish to see my treasure?'

'No, I'll leave that to Sir Ralph and the rector,' Jimbo replied, not admitting he had already seen it. Mr Fitch flicked a switch on his intercom and asked Fenella to come. She led Ralph and Peter away, glancing back to wink at Jimbo while Mr Fitch answered his telephone.

Peter was deeply moved when he saw what Fenella brought out of the safe. He reverently cradled each piece in his hands one by one. 'Why, they're wonderful, just unbelievable. Worthy of a cathedral. So totally splendid. To think no one has been able to enjoy these for over fifty years. It's simply not right.'

Fenella, embarrassed by his obvious admiration for the

pieces, observed, 'They are very beautiful aren't they? You must be very sorry they're being taken away.'

Ralph replied before Peter could answer. 'Not if I can damn well help it.' He glowered at Peter. 'If you won't put up a fight for these, then I shall. I don't remember any of this being in the church, but look at the engravings; this is church property and it's a crime to sell it off.' He watched Peter tenderly tracing the decoration on one of the large altar dishes. Gruffly Ralph said, 'Yes, certainly, this is one he isn't going to win.'

One by one the pieces of silver were carefully rewrapped and returned to the safe. Peter stood up and asked Ralph what he intended to do.

'I shall tell him that he has exactly three days to come to his senses and then I shall act. I shall begin by speaking to the son of a friend of mine. He's an investigative journalist and will be salivating, positively salivating, at the opportunity to dig up dirt about a big City name. Oh, yes, indeed. I shall give it all I've got.' He turned on his heel, and left the office.

Fenella looked alarmed. 'He's not going to challenge Mr Fitch, is he?'

'I rather think he is.'

'I'd stay here then, Rector.'

'I'd better go support him.'

Ralph had walked into Mr Fitch's office without knocking. Jimbo and he were leaning over some papers on his desk, comparing notes. Mr Fitch looked up when he stormed in. 'I beg your pardon, do you have something else to say?'

Ralph went to lean his hands on the desk. They confronted each other like two adversaries in a Roman arena. 'Indeed I do. If you take that silver and sell it, it will be blatant, absolutely blatant, theft and I shall make certain that a highly reputable broadsheet gets all the facts. For heavens sake, man, see sense. Don't make me do it. It's not in my nature, but I *will* act if you persist with the sale. Three clear days,' he held up three fingers, 'three days only, you have. If the silver is not back in the rector's possession by midnight on Thursday, first thing Friday morning I shall ring my contact.'

'I see. The church will pay me its market value, will it?'

Ralph snorted angrily and retorted. 'Don't think you can ride roughshod over me. You've met your match in me, Mr Craddock Fitch. Heed what I say.'

He strode from the office, with Peter in his wake. Jimbo folded up the computer print-outs they'd been looking at and put them in an envelope. As Ralph left, Jimbo said, 'You'd be well advised to listen, he's no fool.'

'He's not coming here and flexing his moribund aristocratic muscle at me. Those days are gone, and gone for good, otherwise *he'd* be standing here in this library instead of *me*.'

Jimbo shook his head sorrowfully. 'Don't make the mistake of underestimating him. He has connections in all the right places, believe me. Unfortunately for you the whole village will be behind him and that, believe it or not, is a power to be reckoned with. Make no mistake.' Jimbo turned to go. 'I'll study these at home. Let you have my opinion as soon as. Good morning.'

Peter and Ralph were waiting in Ralph's Mercedes for Jimbo to emerge. Ralph was gripping the steering wheel so tightly his knuckles were white. Peter was silent. Jimbo got into the rear seat and said after a moment, 'Thank you, Ralph, for being so forthright. It needed to be said.' After a pause he inquired, 'Do you really have a good contact in Fleet Street?'

'Of course. I'll finish him over this. If you have his ear, tell him so.'

'I've told him already.'

'Good. We'll have to hope he has the brains to do the right thing. Otherwise Fitch plc will be kaput.' He revved up the engine, crashed the gears, and they shot down the drive at top speed. Jimbo and Peter both wished they'd elected to walk home.

Jimbo, still pale around the gills after his nightmare drive back to the village, changed in the store room into his butcher's apron, bow tie and boater, grabbed a quick coffee from his customers' coffee machine, and took over behind the till.

For a Monday morning the Store was quite busy. There was a knot of people behind the cereal shelves arguing fiercely. A hold had been put on their shopping and they stood, wirebaskets on their arms, heads nodding, fingers wagging, voices lowered. Jimbo waited patiently; he knew he'd find out shortly what it was all about. They dispersed, finished collecting their groceries, and then came to the till.

Their spokeswoman plunged straight to the point. 'Now Mr Charter-Plackett, there's a tale going round the village that old Fitch up at the Big House has decided he's selling what's rightly ours. Is it true? We understand you've been up there today with the rector and Sir Ralph.'

Faced with such an outright question Jimbo had no alternative but to acknowledge the truth. 'How did you find out?'

'Well, one way and another we've all got relatives or neighbours who work up there. It doesn't take long for news to spread. My Barry was the joiner he asked to take down the panelling. My Barry bloody well knew what had been found, because he dragged the boxes out. What he didn't know was what the intentions were of that high and mighty City gent. 'Cept that's not what our Barry calls him.' She grinned and nudged the woman standing next to her.

'Well, yes, it is true. Sir Ralph has given him an ultimatum.'

'Ultimatum?'

'Yes, an ultimatum. It has all to be in the rector's hands by midnight Thursday or else.'

'Or else what?' a voice at the back of the crowd shouted.

'Or else Sir Ralph is telling the newspapers.'

'Serves him right. Stealing from the church. It's a wonder the heavens don't open and he gets struck by lightning. We all know what happened the last time someone stole from the church. Divine retribution, that's what.'

Jimbo was hesitant about blaming God. 'Steady, I say, steady, I don't think it works like that.'

'I may not go to church like you do, but I do know what's what. The rector, God love 'im, would find an excuse for the devil let alone that old Fitch plc, but we know. Oh, yes, we know what's right.'

'Remember!' said Barry's mother. 'Thursday night's the deadline. Pressure will be brought to bear! All agreed?' There was a general nodding of heads. 'How much is my shopping then, Mr Charter-Plackett? Ten pounds forty-two?' 'Ave you added that up right?' She peered angrily at her till receipt. 'Oh, yes, I'd forgotten about the chops.' As Barry's mother turned to leave she punched the air with her fist and said, 'Remember everybody! It's time for action!' She left the Store with her rallying cry echoing in their ears.

Chapter 7

On the Wednesday morning, just as Linda was about to take her coffee break, an exact fifteen minutes which was not permitted under any circumstances to be shortened by the mistimed arrival of a customer for the post office, Venetia arrived in the Store.

She was shivering. 'Good morning, Venetia!' Jimbo raised his boater. Harriet, who'd been helping her mother in the mail order office, appeared in case Jimbo needed a helping hand in Linda's absence.

Having come to terms at last with Venetia's constant pursuit of any suitable male, including Jimbo, Harriet said cheerfully, 'Hello, Venetia, how's tricks?'

'How's tricks? Oh, golly, it's so beautifully warm in here. Can I stand by the radiator for a while?'

'You're welcome. What's more I'll bring you a coffee. It's freshly made.' Harriet busied herself at the coffee machine. 'Sugar? Milk? Cream?'

'Oh no, black please, no sugar. Got to think of my figure.'

'Well, your thoughtfulness certainly pays dividends.'

'Thanks Jimbo, how kind you are.'

Harriet handed the coffee to her and asked, 'Are we permitted to ask why you are so cold?'

'Something horrendous has happened to the central heating at Turnham House. The electrician says there's an essential part gone wrong called a gizmo or something, and they're in short supply and it could be a week before he gets the part. Jeremy's going spare. He's offered to drive anywhere, however far away, to get it, but the electrician says even the dealers have none in stock and it's to come from Germany. How we shall exist for a whole week without heating I don't know. That huge open fireplace in the hall is brilliant, but it only heats the hall and staircase, nowhere else. Added to which we had a complete blackout of the lights and power last night, so we were groping around with candles for nearly an hour. Crad . . . Mr Fitch is furious.'

She shivered as she drank her coffee. 'Oh! That's wonderful. Come to say the cook's had to go home with the 'flu, Jimbo. They can manage lunch, but Jeremy wants you to do something about dinner and pronto. I volunteered to come down to tell you, because the phones have been on the blink too. It's like a total shut-down. Fenella found the fax hadn't been on all night and she didn't realise it until just now, and she's lost a load of data off the computer. She's tearing her hair out by the handful. Believe you me, we were better off with pens and paper and a messenger boy on a bike.'

Harriet, knowing Jimbo as she did, suspected his complete disregard of Venetia's news meant he knew more than he was saying. She filled the silence by saying, 'Mr Fitch will be none too pleased.'

'No, he's not. In fact he's fuming. I've been trying to calm him down.' She fluffed her hair with her spare hand

and adjusted her headband. 'He's leaving after lunch and says he wants everything in working order before he comes back on Thursday night or heads will roll.'

Jimbo said quickly. 'Is he taking the church silver with him?'

Momentarily Venetia looked guilty, rapidly changing her expression when she saw Jimbo scrutinising her face. 'Oh! I don't know, that's nothing to do with me. I'm not in the office.'

'You may not be in the office, but you do have his ear. Come on, it's vital I know. You owe me.'

She shuffled her feet a little, finished the last of the coffee and said reluctantly, 'He's taking it away on Friday when he goes back to London. That's privileged information.'

'Thanks. I'll make sure there's a replacement cook there by early afternoon. I've a few numbers I can ring. Will you excuse me?' He wandered off into the back.

Harriet served some customers and left Venetia keeping warm by the radiator. Several people stopped to have a word with her, and commiserated about the heating. Harriet had never heard them be so sympathetic to Venetia before. She thought she detected a hint of mockery in their voices.

'You never can tell with all these new-fangled machines, can you? Always going wrong just when there's a cold snap.'

'Fancy, having to come from Germany. Could be a fortnight, even. Well, I never. What bad luck.'

'Let's hope that electrician knows what he's talking about.'

When there was a lull and Harriet had a moment to spare, Venetia said she must be pleased that houses were going to be built on the spare land. 'Be a big increase in trade for you, won't it?'

'Well, I'm being very philosophical about it. It could all be rumour, you know. These things take so long and there's bound to be a lot of opposition.'

'I expect so. Well, I must be off, I've an executive trim class in half an hour. Do you really think it will take a week for the heating to come back on?'

'I've no idea, I really haven't. Come down to get warm any time won't you?'

Linda came back and Harriet went to find Jimbo. 'You were remarkably quiet when Venetia was telling us about the electricity cut. Do you know something I don't know?'

Jimbo took off his boater and stroked his few remaining strands of hair into place. 'Look, I could be completely wrong. It could all be coincidence, but I do know the village are planning a pressure campaign to force Fitch to give the silver back. They really mean business. So I think they've engineered it all deliberately.'

'Help! I didn't think they would dare go to such lengths. I mean, he's not a man to be trifled with is he?'

'No, and I've a feeling this is only the beginning.'

'It'll be effigies and pin sticking next.'

'Now Harriet, you're letting your imagination run away with you. Don't let's get ridiculous.' He placed his hands on her shoulders and kissed her soundly. 'Expectant mothers should be going home for lunch. Off you go.'

'Right then, I'll waddle off.'

Jimbo went up to the Big House in the early afternoon; he'd tried telephoning but couldn't get through, and he began to worry that his meticulous planning had gone awry. As he drove through the gates, he realised there was something fastened to each of the stone pillars either side of the drive. He braked rapidly, reversed out into the road again and saw two placards with thick red lettering on them. One said 'PUBLIC ENEMY NUMBER ONE', the other 'SNAKE IN THE GRASS'. He chuckled and then had a struggle with his conscience; after all he had a lot to lose. Should he take them down? But Jimbo decided that as Fitch had already left they would do no harm, and continued on his way up to the house.

But Mr Fitch hadn't left, he was standing outside the front door. There were several men with him, all in smart business suits. They were talking animatedly, with Mr Fitch the centre of it all. Jimbo got out and out of courtesy went to pass the time of day.

'Good afternoon, Charter-Plackett.'

'Good afternoon, just come to check my new cook's arrived and everything is shipshape.'

'Shipshape! Will anything be shipshape ever again? Damnation! The place is cursed.'

'Cursed?'

Mr Fitch almost exploding with annoyance, turned on his heel and disappeared inside the house. Jimbo raised his eyebrows questioningly at one of the young men.

'Wanted to leave straight after lunch but all his tyres are flat.' The young man had difficulty in restraining the smile which had crept to the corners of his mouth.

'Well, couldn't he borrow someone else's?'

'No one but him has a Rolls, and he doesn't want to travel in anything less. He's waiting for the odd job chappie to pump them up again with his foot pump. But it's taking a long time.'

'Ah! Right!' Jimbo nodded to them all and strode into

the house. It was cold. Fenella was wearing her coat. 'Mr Charter-Pla . . . '

'Stop!'

'Jimbo then, we're so cold. You can't repair boilers can you?'

'I have many, many valuable attributes, but repairing boilers is not one of them.'

'I bet you have! You'll have to tell me about them sometime! Have you come to see Mr Fitch? You'd better not have.'

'No, just come to check the kitchen's firing on all cylinders.'

'It isn't, there's a dispute about the new cook and they're all thinking of downing tools.'

'They'd better not.' He stormed through the green baize door into the kitchen. His staff were all clustered round the new cook and were in the process of voting on a decision.

'All those in favour then!' Using all his powers of persuasion he told them that as Mr Fitch was leaving, the only ones who would suffer from their downing tools were the trainees, so there was nothing to be gained. Added to which he wouldn't pay any one of them a single penny for hours not worked. They agreed not to strike. They were obviously doing it on purpose, but their faces were poker straight and none broke ranks and confessed it was all part of a campaign. He gave them one of his renowned pep talks, a combination of underlying threat mixed with morale-boosting statements about the valuable service they were giving, about image and confidence, about loyalty and pride, about the importance of the role each of them played, they weren't simply cogs in a machine et cetera. By the time he'd finished he seriously considered offering his services as guest lecturer at the house. He came out and saw Mr Fitch leave in his Rolls, his chauffeur speeding the car away in a flurry of scattered gravel. Oh God! The placards. He'd see the placards. Too late now.

By Thursday morning Peter had to admit to himself that he coveted the silver in Mr Fitch's safe. Each time he looked at the altar he could imagine how beautiful it would look on display there. He knew exactly where he would stand that huge candlestick, right there, no a little over to one side nearer the choir stalls, no would it . . . He stopped himself in his tracks. What was he doing? Expending energy on mere trivialities; it mattered not one jot how beautiful the church looked – well it did, but not to that extent. It was all very unedifying. What mattered most was the souls of his congregation. That was what should be at the forefront of his mind, not moaning about how to improve the appearance of the church for the greater glory of his ego. He felt ashamed of himself, and tried Caroline's patience by discussing the problem ceaselessly in the kitchen after breakfast. She took a much more commonsense approach.

'For heaven's sake don't torture yourself about it. The man is stealing. Full stop. He knows he is, we know he is, and it has to be stopped. When we get it back, *then* the decision can be taken as to whether or not it is sold or we keep it. The responsibility of keeping it safe is mind boggling, but there you are. Now, Alex is waiting for you to play football and Beth wants to play too, and she has a doll which needs mending, so please, darling, apply your mind to that and stop fretting.'

'What shall I do if he doesn't bring it back?'

'Report him to the police. At five minutes past mid-night. Off you go, Sylvia and I have work to do and you're cluttering the place up with your moral dilemmas.'

The telephone rang in the rectory at half past eight that night. Peter answered it.

'Good evening. Turnham Malpas Rectory. Peter Harris speaking.'

'Fitch. Craddock Fitch. Can you come to Turnham House?'

'Yes, I can.'

'Now?'

'Yes.'

'Thank you. Come straight in. I'll be in the library.'

On his way up the drive in the dark, Peter's way was barred by the estate Land Rover parked on the road. He got out. In the headlights he could see Jeremy and two men, whom Peter recognised as village residents, struggling with what appeared to be a body hanging from a low branch of a tree growing about six feet from the edge of the drive.

One of the men touched his cap and grinned saying 'Good evening, Rector. Just busy moving this. We'll be out of your way in a minute. Shan't be long.'

Jeremy, through tight lips, said, 'I'll get the damned fools who did this, and when I get my hands on 'em I'll throttle 'em.'

Peter peered at the body. It was dangling from a rope. Its head, topped by what appeared to be a mophead sprayed with silver paint, hung forward, the rope around the neck. A navy suit jacket covered the well stuffed rag body, and stabbed straight through where its heart would be were two thick, silver-coloured knitting needles. From its neck hung a placard with two words written on it: 'FITCH! THIEF!' A torch had been tied onto the branch so that the rag effigy was illuminated. It couldn't be missed by anyone going past. When they'd cut it down and taken the torch off the branch, they stuffed it in the Land Rover. The two men winked at Peter as they jumped in beside Jeremy, who sped off towards the house as fast as he could.

Mr Fitch was waiting in the library and offered Peter a drink, but he refused. Mr Fitch poured himself a whisky.

Please, Rector, please sit down.' Mr Fitch sat in his desk chair. 'I suppose you saw my effigy?'

'I did.'

'Since Tuesday it has been mayhem here.'

'I did hear something about you having problems.'

'Indeed.' He paused to sip his whisky. 'I am un-accustomed to not getting my own way. But it would appear I am thwarted this time by a pack of country yokels not worth a ha'penny.' He snapped his fingers in a derisive gesture. 'If I sold the silver, the money I would get would be a drop in the ocean. That's not the point. It's the principle. What I buy is mine, or rather my company's.'

'You may snap your fingers at them, but to me they are my prime care. They are good, honest, hard-working people who instinctively know, without really knowing how, what is right. I owe them a lot. They have supported me through a very difficult time in my life, not saying anything but just being there, shoulder to shoulder like some invisible army. If you do what you intend, nothing will go right here. They'll see it doesn't.'

'I can bus people in.'

'Of course, there are ways round it. But sell what they feel is rightly theirs and somehow they will get their revenge. They will never accept you. Never.'

'You talk as if they are one body.'

'They are in a kind of a way. They and generations before them have lived here in this place. It is theirs. Not yours. Not mine. Theirs. We're here on sufferance till we've lived here fifty years and more. Imagine, if you can, the feeling of taking communion from a cup that has been used by one's ancestors for over two hundred years. Think of living in a cottage which was standing when the plague came. Worshipping in a church which has stood here for almost seven hundred years. What a sense of permanence. What a sense of history. What a sense of *belonging*. I feel deeply privileged to be allowed to be at the heart of these people.'

Mr Fitch swirled his whisky round his glass. He finished off the last drops and, resting his elbows on his desk, looked straight at Peter.

'What you're saying is if we are to keep going here, I've to kowtow to these yokels.'

'No, I am not saying that. I'm saying do what is right. If you kowtow, as you call it, it won't work. They are not fools and they'll know if they're being patronised.'

Mr Fitch pondered for a while, taking his time putting papers and files on his desk into neat straight lines. Peter watched his face and endeavoured to understand what he was thinking. Suddenly Mr Fitch appeared to make up his mind. He took some keys from his pocket. With a wry smile on his face he said, 'Then, my first step on this road to acceptance will be to return the church silver to its rightful place. Hopefully doing this will put an end to the chaos here. I don't mind admitting to you that effigy made me blanch when I saw it. Positively mediaeval!' Peter thought he saw him shudder.

Mr Fitch helped Peter stow the boxes in his estate car. He

slammed down the door and turned to shake hands. 'I see you've got two safety seats in the back.'

'Yes, they're for my twins.'

'Lucky man. Goodnight.'

'Goodnight, and thank you.'

Chapter 8

Dawn was just breaking when Malcolm the milkman brought his van to a standstill beside Jimmy's garden fence. 'Morning Mr Glover. You're up and about in good time. Not often I see you on the go so early nowadays.'

'No, well, I've got a project in 'and. Are yer wanting yer money?'

'If yer like, but it can wait till next week if yer busy.'

'I'll go inside and get it. I've turned over a new leaf since I 'ad that big win.'

'Are you still filling 'em in?'

'No, I'm not. I'm not greedy. 'Ang on.'

Malcolm waited while Jimmy went inside to get his money. Beside the fence was a big fourteen-pound hammer. Stacked neatly against the wall of the house were ready-made timber panels, which looked as though they would make a shed when put together.

After Jimmy had paid him, Malcolm couldn't resist asking what Jimmy's intentions were.

'Making a new chicken house.'

'But you've got one already.'

'I know I 'ave, but that's coming down and a new one,

nearer the house, is going up.'

'I see. Why?'

'Wait and see.' Jimmy turned away and began work on the rough ground about twelve feet nearer the house than the old chicken run. Malcolm had to leave it at that, as Jimmy obviously had no intention of revealing what he had in mind.

Vera and Pat tolerated the hammering for most of the morning before coming out to protest.

Pat shouted across Vera's garden, 'Look, it's grand to see you working hard, but 'ow much longer is this banging going on for? My head's absolutely spinning.'

'And mine as well. What are yer doing, Jimmy?'

'You'll see, you'll see.'

'Making a new chicken run by the looks of it. What will yer do with the old one?'

'Knock it down.'

'Why?'

'Wait and see. Yer going to 'ave the surprise of your life shortly.'

'That'll be the day. Well, if yer won't tell us then, when this surprise appears I for one won't *be* surprised, I'll ignore it.'

'Do that then.'

'Winning that money 'as gone to your 'ead, Jimmy Glover, that's what.'

Flick Charter-Plackett stopped to have a word with him after lunch.

'Hello, Mr Glover. Will you sponsor me for Brownies? I've got my list here and a pen.' She held up a smart clipboard she'd purloined from Jimbo's office.

Jimmy leant on his fourteen-pound hammer, pushed his cap to the back of his head, and asked her what she would have to do for it.

'It's a sponsored silence. I've to promise not to say a word for a whole hour and then Brown Owl signs my sheet and I can collect the money.'

'You! Keep silent for one whole hour? You can't keep silent for one whole minute!'

'I can if I try. My Daddy gave me fifty pence for keeping quiet for one whole hour when we set off on our holidays. He said he needed peace and quiet to pull himself together after he'd struggled to organise us all. So Fergus and Finlay and me, we sat in the back of the car and never spoke for an hour. Mummy said it was like heaven. So I can do it.'

''Ow much 'as your Dad promised?'

'Well, he's promised five pence a minute, but that's because he thinks with all those girls there I won't manage it, but I shall. But you can give me one pence a minute if you like. That's what Mrs Wright next door has promised me.'

'If she's promised you one pence I'll give you two pence. 'Ave you asked Mrs Duckett?'

'I'm going there next, she wasn't in when I called before.'

'Put her name down and I'll give you two pence a minute for 'er and don't bother to ask 'er, right? And don't let on?'

Flick nodded sagely, 'Oh right, I understand. That's very thoughtful of you, Mr Glover.' After she'd carefully written in the names and amounts, Flick asked Jimmy what he was doing.

'Well now, Flick, it could be said that my moment has arrived. There comes a time in a man's life when he has to take steps and this is it for me. I'm not telling you what I'm doing because it wouldn't be fair to expect you not to tell and I don't want anyone knowing. They've always thought of me as a daft useless old bugg— chap but I'm going to show 'em and not half.' He grinned at her, pulled one of her plaits in a friendly way and went back to work.

'I've never thought of you as a daft useless old what you said. I've always liked you, Mr Glover.'

'In that case then, we're friends for life.' He shook her hand and she left smiling.

By evening the entire village had grown weary of Jimmy's banging. Worse was to come, because before it got dark, he knocked down the old run with much gusto and then commenced on the fence. His chickens, objecting to their abrupt removal to new quarters, squabbled and squawked, adding to the general din.

No one except Georgie knew what he was up to and she refused to declare his secret. 'He told me the night he knew he'd won, and I've not told a soul, not even Bryn. It's Jimmy's secret and all will be revealed shortly. Now what can I get you?' Before the evening was over Georgie had made this declaration several times. Every customer who came in wanted to know; having put up with the din all day they felt justified in inquiring.

'Winning them pools 'as sent 'im crackers. That secretive he is.'

'He's always been secretive, it's nothing new. I remember when his wife died, what was 'er name? He spoke to nobody for months. Yer couldn't even say 'ow sorry yer were. 'E shut up like a clam.'

'How much money did he win, 'as he told you?'

'No, and not likely to, after I opposed him about his rabbit snaring.'

''Eard about these houses the council's building? Two hundred they say.'

'Two hundred? On that bit of land, never, they'll be like rabbit hutches.'

'I've heard they found out it's Sir Ralph's land and it's him building 'em.'

'Never! There's that many rumours flying about.'

'More houses, better chance of keeping the school open, more business for the Store and we need that, can't trip into Culworth every time yer need a packet of tea, could do us all good.'

'Well, I disagree. We don't want all them houses whosoever's building 'em. We got our own way about that church silver and we'll get our own way about this. Mark my words. With all our talk we still haven't found out what Jimmy Glover's doing. Whatever it is, he's either gone cracked or at last he's waking up to the twentieth century.'

It poured with rain the following day, so no one noticed Jimmy getting on the breakfast-time bus; they were all inside keeping dry.

Around five o'clock a bright red, brand new Vauxhall Cavalier rolled gently into the village. The driver signalled right to turn down Stocks Row in front of the weekenders' cottages, and then quickly signalled left and humped and bumped onto the bottom end of Jimmy's garden, now free of the fence and the chicken run.

It was Jimmy who got out of it. It was Jimmy who got out a handkerchief from his inside pocket and wiped his finger marks off the door. Though it was raining, it was Jimmy who strolled slowly round the car, relishing its colour and the complete and glorious newness of it. He got the key from the ignition and opened up the boot, but he had to close it quickly because of the rain wetting the inside of it. He got back in and, sitting in the driver's seat, he fiddled with the radio. Suddenly ferociously loud music hammered its way through the windows. Jimmy hurriedly twisted knobs and pressed buttons and the wipers began working furiously, the horn sounded, the lights went on and off until he got the noise under control. Before long, despite the rain, a small group of curious villagers collected. Georgie, tapped on the driver's window and signalled to him to wind it down.

'Beautiful, really beautiful. What a good choice.'

'Do yer think so? Isn't it great. I'm that pleased with it.'

'Since when did you learn to drive, Jimmy?' Vera asked.

'Learned years ago when I worked on Home Farm for a spell, and I've kept me licence up to date all these years.'

Pat said, 'We'd better warn everybody then if it's that long since yer drove! But Jimmy, what will yer use it for? It does seem an extravagance.' She trailed her fingers along its smooth glossy paintwork, enjoying the rich feel of it.

He got out of the car and locked the door. 'Central locking, yer notice. All mod cons.'

'Well?' asked Pat.

'I 'eard that one of the minicab drivers at Culworth Station had got finished, so I went there to see about it, and I've got miself 'is job. I start this week. This is an investment, this is.' He patted the car and then got out his handkerchief and wiped the bodywork in case he'd left any fingerprints.

'Well, I never. Jimmy Glover with a regular job. 'Ope you won't be coming 'ome from work at all hours and waking us up.'

'Yer never know.'

Saying that, he turned on his heel and walked into his house.

Pat swallowed hard. It was difficult not to be envious of such good luck. Ah well, egg and chips again tonight, and let Dean or Michelle grumble and they'd get the sharp edge of her tongue.

★

A week after starting work with the Culworth Cab Company Jimmy spent his only free evening in The Royal Oak. As he took his first frothing pint from Alan Crimble he said, "Ow's that old banger of yours Alan? Still holding together is it?'

'Just about. Lady Luck doesn't come to us all yer know, Mr Glover. She's old, I know, but I love her. Living in this Godforsaken place, I 'ad to do something about my own transport. The last bus from Culworth gets here at six o'clock and what use is that to a young man with a sex life?'

Jimmy wiped the froth from his lips and said, 'Wouldn't know about sex life in Culworth. Didn't think they 'ad any.'

'Seeing as you're doing your taxi job now, I thought perhaps you'd know. That new night club, yer know in Deansgate, The Force . . . '

'That's a daft name and not 'alf.'

'Daft it might be, but it's great.'

'Anyways, last time I see'd your car, it struck me it needed servicing. Got to keep 'em well looked after, yer know.'

'Servicing? The money I get paid 'ere you couldn't afford to service a push bike.'

'Dangerous yer know, Alan, dangerous.' Jimmy took his pint to his favourite seat and settled down to wait for some company.

Pat Duckett came in. Jimmy watched her order her drink. Her shoulders were slumped and he noticed that the cheerful face she usually wore had been left at home.

'Hello, Jimmy.' Pat sat down on the settle opposite him and sipped her port and lemon.

'Need cheering up? Kids is it?'

'No, mi Dad. He's got his notice this morning. Job gone

'cos of council cuts and he has two months to get out of his house, goes with the job yer see. He's never saved any money so guess where he's coming?'

'I'm sorry, Pat.'

'Not as sorry as I am.' She dolefully took a sip of her drink and changed the subject. 'We've won over the church silver, haven't we? It was me found out, yer know.'

'Oh, right. Busybodying were yer?'

'No, just working up there, waitressing, the day they found it. Couldn't let 'im get away with that, could we? The old sod. Rich as hell and still wants to make more money. Couldn't 'elp but laugh about that dummy they hung up on that tree. 'Ope it frightened him to death. Did the trick, didn't it?'

'Do you know who did it?'

Pat looked him in the eye and said, 'No.'

'Yer lying, I can tell.'

'So?'

'You weren't the only one who brought pressure to bear.'

'Why, what did you do?'

'Just passing the bus stop when some of them students got off and asked me the way to Turnham House. All la di da they was. Plums in their mouths an' that. So I directed 'em down Royal Oak Road. I laughed all morning about that.'

'Jimmy! Yer never! That was a rotten trick, that was.'

'I know. It was the only thing I could think of to show my support.'

'Good for you.'

'Have they decided what to do with it?'

'Not that I know of, but then I'm not privy to what goes on at the church, am I?'

'No, yer not. I'll tell yer a tale, shall I? To cheer you up.'

'Go on then.'

'It's about mi job. I could work day and night seven days a week I could, yer know. The Cab Company's making money hand over fist. There's ten of us working from there, and the number of punters is amazing. All hours of the day and night.'

Pat leant forward and said they couldn't be respectable if they wanted a cab in the middle of the night. She said it hoping for some juicy story of night life in Culworth.

'There's lots o' folks needing taxis in the middle of the night. They come out of that night club, yer know that place in Deansgate, and want a lift home 'cos the buses 'ave stopped, or they come off trains in the middle of the night when they've been abroad. It's amazin' what goes on, or they've had too much to drink and 'ave to leave their cars and get a taxi 'ome. All sorts.'

'Bet you meet some funny customers, Jimmy.'

'Yer right there. Thursday night this chap got in, drunk as a lord he was, wanted to go to a house out near the race course. All of twenty miles. We were miles from anywhere, and he asks to get out for a minute 'cos he needed to 'ave a . . . well, relieve himself. He never came back. I waited and waited, then I went to see where he was. But he wasn't behind the bushes where I'd last seen 'im and I never saw him again'.

'What about yer money?'

'I didn't get it, but 'e did leave something behind.'

'What?'

'A set of false teeth on the back seat – and they weren't even clean!'

Pat shouted at him. 'Oh Jimmy, what a disgusting tale that is. Is them them that you've got in now?' She roared with laughter.

'No, they didn't fit!'

After the laughter had died down Pat asked him if he was making money at it.

'Oh yes, never made as much in mi life. Not a fortune, 'cos there's the running expenses of mi car to be deducted, but yes, I'm going to be a well-set-up young man shortly.'

'That's what I need, money. It sounds lovely having your own roof over your head but you've got the upkeep, painting it and that, and I've no money to spare for that. I don't know what I'm going to do, I really don't. Better get back to the kids. Thanks for making me laugh. 'Night.'

Chapter 9

Ralph had made no effort to dispel the rumours which were rife in the village. He'd been approached several times by villagers, all hoping he would lead the protest against the council building the houses. All he'd said was 'I don't think the council will be building them', but hadn't enlightened them any further. He couldn't until he had resolved a problem. Namely persuading Muriel he was doing the right thing. She was still very unhappy about the whole affair. Ralph, sitting with her before the fire one late spring morning, was debating what to do about the impasse they had arrived at. Having been a bachelor for all his life until this last year he was unaccustomed to having his decisions queried, but because of his love for Muriel, he knew he would not have a moment's peace until she willingly came round to his point of view. To sweeten the pill, that was the problem.

'You know, Muriel, my dear, I've been thinking, you have a very good eye for things beautiful haven't you? Would it be an imposition if I asked you to co-operate with the architects and feed them some of your ideas?'

'I haven't got any ideas, Ralph. I don't want to have any

ideas, truly I don't and I'm sorry to be so difficult but that's how I feel.' She avoided looking at him.

'What I thought was you could make sure they designed the outside of the houses, certainly the ones nearest Shepherd's Hill and Stocks Row, so that they would blend in with the old cottages already here. We don't want red-brick three-bedroom semis going up, do we? That would be appalling, and not at all what I have in mind.'

'If you hadn't thought of the idea in the first place, you wouldn't be appalled because there'd be nothing to be appalled about. I'm afraid the renowned Templeton charm is not going to work. My mind is quite set.'

Ralph sighed. Timid people could be so damned stubborn when they put their minds to it.

'If I called it Hipkin Close, would that help?'

'When Jimbo made Harriet so cross by starting the tearoom without consulting her first, he tried calling it "Harriet's Tearoom" to persuade her not to oppose it. It's a pity it had to close, isn't it? I did like it in there. Well, it didn't work with her and it won't work with me. Oh dear. I'm sorry, Ralph. You need my support and I should be giving it to you, not opposing you at every turn. I'm very sorry.'

'That's all right, my dear, you do have a right to your own opinions. What do you think to Neville Neal?' She paused for a moment before she answered. He waited, intrigued by the conflicting emotions in her face.

'As Church Treasurer he does an excellent job, but he's not quite a *gentleman*, is he?'

Ralph chuckled. 'I knew I could trust you to hit the nail on the head. However, I'll see if he has any advice on how to proceed with our ideas for Hipkin Gardens. That sounds better doesn't it, Hipkin Gardens, it will be a kind of memorial to your father, won't it? Your family were gardeners for generations so Gardens is ideal. It's much better than Hipkin Close. I'm going to ring Neville now to see if I can get to know anything, he always seems to know what the council is up to.'

'I'll make you some coffee, you can drink it while you talk. The business side is best left to you.'

Ralph was put through to Neville in his office and he began a long and fruitful conversation about planning permission. He became so involved in his discussion that he didn't realise that Muriel had been standing in the doorway listening. When he replaced the receiver he glanced up to find her glaring at him, her face scarlet and stormy and her eyes sparking angrily.

'Hipkin Gardens.'

'Hipkin Gardens?'

'Yes, Hipkin Gardens is *not* going to be built by a den of thieves. I won't have it.' She stamped her foot. Ralph stood up.

'Muriel, I assure you . . . '

'No, Ralph. I heard what you said. Oh yes I did! I don't want to hear any more about paying councillors and scratching people's backs for them to get you what you want. If it's to bear my name and my father's, it's to be done right.'

Ralph went to draw her into the room. He took her arm and said, 'Sit here my dear, I don't like you to be upset and angry, you're quite mistaken.'

'Mistaken? I'm not. I heard you saying "and how about if it was one hundred houses". I heard you, I did, I heard you, and what tricks you would get up to to get permission. I heard you! It will all be spoilt if we have to be underhand. I'm surprised at you and very, very disappointed. This

84

behaviour is not at all in keeping with your position.' She flopped down into the chair Ralph offered her and then began trembling with distress. 'Oh dear, I'm so sorry, but I mean what I said.' She searched for a handkerchief but finally Ralph lent her his.

Ralph shook his head. Muriel was in tears.

'Muriel! Please!'

'All I came in for was to bring your coffee.' Tears trickled down her cheeks. Rather petulantly she cried, 'And I'm glad I did. I won't have it Ralph, I simply won't. I want it all to be lovely and great fun, and all it's going to be is nasty and horrid and small minded, and then there won't be any pleasure in doing good for the village at all. And no one will like us, and we shall have to leave, and that dreadful Mr Fitch will be in your place.' She dried her tears and said accusingly, 'Why *are* you talking about a hundred houses?'

'It was him talking about a hundred houses, and I went along with it to see how much I could learn about what to do.'

Muriel signalled her disbelief by lifting her chin and turning away her head. 'I can see which way the land lies, you're getting carried away with this idea.'

Ralph pulled a chair across the carpet and placed it in front of Muriel's. Taking her hand in his he said, 'I won't have this whole lovely idea spoiled for you, not on any account. I'd rather not go through with it than have you upset like this. I was only trying out ideas with Neville, about agreeing to one thing in order to get one's own way about another. You've quite misunderstood my conversation. You're right to be indignant. We're going to go about it the honourable way, I promise you that.' He smiled reassuringly at her.

Muriel smiled through her tears and said, 'I shall keep

you to it, Ralph, I really shall. I won't be put off.'

'I know, dear. People like Neville need someone like you to remind them of the honourable way to do things. I promise you faithfully I shall do things the way you want them done, otherwise I couldn't live with myself. I love you, you see.'

Muriel kissed Ralph and said, 'Thank you for coming back to Turnham Malpas. The years ahead would have been very bleak without you.'

'Thank you for saying "yes". It makes everything I do so much more worthwhile. Let's go have lunch in The Royal Oak? They tell me Bryn has got a new home-brewed ale in, and I should like to try it.' He smiled pleadingly at her, trying to make amends.

Muriel took his hand and held it to her cheek. 'I always thought this Templeton charm business was a lot of tosh, but it isn't, is it? You've won me round. Yes, I'll come, but only on condition that you don't bring up the subject of the houses, I can't bear it. Please?'

'Cross my heart and hope to die.'

But they had no alternative. Three people came up to him in the dining room, promising their support when he decided to start a petition or demonstration or whatever it was he thought would be the best move. 'After all you helped us win the battle with that old Fitch, if we all stand together we'll stop the council too, won't we?'

Muriel blushed furiously and made a show of eating her lasagne so as to dissociate herself from the conversation. When they'd said their piece and left the dining room she muttered to Ralph, 'We shouldn't have come. I knew it, we shouldn't have. We'll have to leave the village. They won't let you build. They won't. Oh dear.'

Quietly Ralph said, 'My dear, please. They'll guess

something's the matter if you cry.'

'Oh yes, they will, won't they? I shall pull myself together.'

'I shan't let bad blood occur. Believe me. I won't let it happen. You can rely on me.'

'Of course I can. Yes, of course.'

'Anyway it's not official yet, so everyone is jumping the gun.'

Muriel took a sip of her wine and said, 'When we've finished here I've to go to the Store for one or two things, and you're needing stamps, aren't you? You go on home, I shan't be long.'

'Another drink?'

'No, thank you. How is the ale?'

'Excellent. Bryn's a much better landlord than Mac and Betty ever were. Much more style and much more knowledgeable.'

Ralph went home and Muriel continued round the green to the Store. It was very quiet in there; besides someone at the post office counter she was the only customer. She wandered around the shelves choosing what she fancied. That was one of the lovely things about being married to Ralph; she didn't need to worry about every penny she spent. Though she wasn't foolish, of course, that wouldn't be right but . . . She was standing between the two racks of cards and stationery when she overheard the customer talking to Linda at the post office counter.

'And now, I want my pension and I'm collecting my neighbour's as well, she's signed whatever she has to sign, she told me. Bad leg she 'as and not 'alf. Come up like a balloon. She can't walk a step. Three second-class stamps as well, please. June's a right month for birthdays in our family. I dread it coming round. Talking of dread, 'ave you 'eard what I 'eard this morning?'

'Tell me.'

The speaker leant her elbow on the edge of the counter and said, 'I've heard it on good authority that it's Sir Ralph yer know, building the houses on that land when they pull the chapel down, and not the council at all. There's everyone thinking, no, certain, he's getting up a petition against it and all the time it's 'im 'imself. Greedy, that's what. 'As all that money and still he has to make more. These rich people are never satisfied. Yer've a bad cough Linda, and it's affected yer eyes as well, yer keep winking. Are you sure you should be at work?'

Muriel heard Linda whispering and then the speaker said loudly. 'Eavesdroppers never 'ear good of themselves.'

Muriel emerged from between the shelves and, keeping as calm as she could in the circumstances, said in a sharp tone, 'My husband isn't greedy. He may not be Lord of the Manor now, but he still has the interests of the village at heart. He wouldn't dream of doing anything to the detriment of the village, he loves it. He's not interested in making money. Please remember that.' She drew herself up, feeling not unlike a bantam squaring up for a fight.

'Beg yer pardon, I'm sure. But from where I'm standing that's what it looks like.'

'Well, it just isn't so.'

'Certainly made a change to you, Muriel Hipkin, being married to money. Wouldn't say boo to a goose before. Oh, no! Very shy and retiring yer were then. Different story now, I see. Well, you're not throwing your weight about with me. Anyway, time will tell who's right. But if he's making money out of it, I shall be at the front with a placard protesting!'

'There won't be any need for a protest. I shall see to that.'

The customer began backing off. 'Well, right then. Be seeing yer, Linda. Good afternoon, *Lady* Templeton.'

Muriel nearly decided to run home, but she'd promised Ralph the stamps so she would look silly if she left now. Linda looked very embarrassed when Muriel appeared at the grille.

'Ten first-class stamps please, Linda. Don't worry yourself, dear, I'm not going to bite your head off too. Some people can't stand change, that's what it is.'

'But Lady Templeton, is he really going to build these houses? Someone said they would be red brick with them nasty patio windows and that, and cost a fortune so village people couldn't buy them. They say it's all because he wants to make a lot of money. But Sir Ralph's not like that, is he?'

'Linda, not even my husband knows if it is going to be possible, so it's all speculation. But take it from me if they do get built they won't be for sale, they'll be to rent.'

'Oh, that would be lovely. My sister, the one who's just got married, had to move to the grotty end of Culworth 'cos she couldn't afford to buy. What a good idea.'

'Thank you, Linda, I'm glad you agree it's a good idea. How much do I owe? Can I pay for these cards here too?'

'Oh yes, I'll take for stationery but everything else at the other till please. Three pounds seventy-five, please. Oh, that's correct, good. I'm short of change.'

On her way home Muriel went into the church and knelt to pray. She prayed mostly for understanding about Ralph's plans. She prayed to be a good wife. She prayed that the village would understand what he was trying to do. There was no doubt about it, she'd have to support this idea of his. It was all to the good. She was sure now. When she'd finished she sat in the pew contemplating life and how lucky she was. She went home to tell him so.

'Are you busy, dear?'

'I shall be glad of a break. Come in and sit down.'

'Ralph, I have realised today how lucky I am. I've been in church having a word, and then I sat thinking about you and what you plan to do. I'd found myself saying in the Store that some people can't stand change. That used to be me, you know. I couldn't stand change. I've had to speak out in defence of you, I was so angry about what someone in the Store was saying. So I spoke up. It's not like me at all, is it?' Ralph shook his head. 'Then Linda said her sister had had to move away because she couldn't afford to buy a house in the village like she wanted to. So that's a possible family of children for the school and the church which we have now lost. We've got to stem the exodus, haven't we?'

'Yes.'

'So, I've been thinking, there isn't any suitable land anywhere else, is there? They certainly wouldn't allow building on farm land, would they?'

'No.'

'So, houses to rent within the village would be an excellent idea, and it's the only piece of land available so close. I know we shall cause a lot of trouble doing it, but in the end it will all be to the good. There!'

Ralph stood up and went to take hold of her hand.

'Muriel, my dear, you are wonderful. I'm delighted you see it my way. You can keep your eagle eye on the planning. I'm not sure how it will work out, we'll have to see what the council think.'

'I don't want horrid council houses on it, Ralph!'

'But if it means houses to rent, then perhaps that will be the best way to go about it. We'll see, we'll see.' Ralph bent his head to kiss her cheek. He smiled down at her and said, 'Best day's work I ever did, coming back and marrying you. Do you know that?'

'Best day's work I did too. Let's get Pericles and walk round Hipkin Gardens, shall we, and do a bit of planning?'

'Lovely idea. Come along Pericles. Walkies! You're getting an extra outing today.' Pericles rose stiffly from his favourite position by the french windows, shook himself and wagged his tail.

'How old is Pericles now, Muriel?'

'Twelve.'

'Living on borrowed time, then.'

'Oh Ralph, don't say that in front of him, he might understand.'

'I know Pericles is clever, but he's not a philosopher.'

'No, you're right he isn't, and you do right to prepare me for him . . . well, going to glory.'

Chapter 10

'Now look Harriet, if you wish I shall cancel this trip, and stay at home.'

'Under no circumstances, James Charter-Plackett, do you cancel! You can't let them down like that at the eleventh hour. I may be about to give birth but I still have a brain left. Our business would fold if you cancelled.'

'I'm sure the staff could do it without me.'

'And I'm sure they couldn't. Heavens above man, I've three weeks still to go. Three whole weeks. Now. Off you go. Mother's here, Caroline's just across the road and anyway I'm going out for the evening. You'll be back the day after tomorrow.'

'I know but . . . Where are you going tonight, then?'

'You've forgotten it's Caroline's Coffee and Gâteau Evening at the rectory in aid of the refurbishment of the small church hall. Remember? You donated a gâteau?'

'Oh right, yes. I'd forgotten. A right hen party that's going to be. What about the children?'

'Mother's coming.'

He smoothed his hand across his chin and said, 'You will take care?'

'Of course. Get along man. I've checked the food, everything's there. Just the things to get out of the freezer and you're away.'

'You're brilliant. Thanks for all you do. When the baby gets here, I don't want to see you anywhere near the business for at least three months. I've got these new people organised, thank heavens there's a lot of unemployed, and we shall manage very nicely.'

'Don't, you're making me feel redundant.' Harriet kissed him, and pushed him out of the door. 'See you when you get back.'

'I'll ring.'

'Got your phone?'

'Yes!' Jimbo raced out of the house, leaving Harriet shaking her head at him.

She was looking forward to the Coffee Evening. It might be her last outing for months. Jimbo had a dread of leaving very young babies with babysitters, and she knew once it had arrived they'd have to entertain at home if they needed company. She'd caught him one day poring over a news-paper article about cot deaths. She'd been expecting Finlay at the time, and he'd looked up with tears in his eyes and said 'I can hardly bear to read about this. God help us if we ever, ever, have this to face.' Harriet had stood beside him and cradled his head against her body. He'd put his arms round her and hugged her tightly and they'd said no more about it, but she knew he still carried the dread. So yes, Caroline, here I come.

Muriel arrived early at the coffee evening, as she always did at any function she attended.

'I know I'm the first one but I thought I might give you a hand. Here's my gâteau, it's Ralph's favourite. I hope I've not gone over the top with the lemon, he loves it really sharp but of course not everyone does, do they?'

'Come in Muriel. Come and put it on the dining table. It looks absolutely splendid. Sylvia and I have organised everything, there's nothing to do except look charming.'

'If there's nothing to do now, I'll stay behind afterwards and help clear up. Ralph's away visiting a friend at the moment so I shall be quite glad to stay. I'm surprised how lonely it feels being on my own. Before I married I never noticed being alone, but now I do. Doesn't the table look beautiful! Where did you get these gâteaux? They look marvellous.'

'Some are from friends, one I've made, this one Sylvia's made and Jimbo gave me the other one. I hope plenty of people turn up or I shall have a freezer full of cake, not that Peter would mind.'

'Is he here this evening?'

'No, he's playing squash at the club in Culworth. I've turfed him out for the evening. Time he got away from the parish and nappies for a while.'

The door bell rang again and Caroline excused herself while she went to answer it. Muriel heard her shout. 'Venetia! How lovely that you could come, and you've brought a gâteau, how kind, I didn't expect it you know, you're supposed to be here to eat them.'

'Thank you for inviting me, I really was thrilled. You're more than kind.'

'Not at all, I'm pleased you could make it. Come in the dining room.'

Venetia came in wearing a sizzlingly spicy orange trouser suit. Only Venetia, with her jet-black hair and well tanned skin, could have carried it off. Anyone else would have been obliterated by the powerful colour. Muriel almost wished

94

she was wearing sunglasses.

'Hello, Venetia, how are you?'

'Very well, thank you, Lady Templeton. Is Sir Ralph here?'

'No, it's ladies only tonight, I'm afraid.'

'Pity, he's so charming and so kind.'

Caroline showed her to an armchair. 'Do sit down, Venetia, I'll put your gâteau here in the middle. It is perfectly splendid, you must be very gifted to be able to make this. I don't know how you manage to fit everything in, Jimbo says it's very busy up at the Big House.'

'Oh, I didn't make it. I was in Culworth at the sports shop getting some things we need for the leisure complex when I spotted that new cake shop that's opened opposite and I couldn't resist. Yes, we are busy. Very busy in fact. Jeremy is in his element in charge of the estate and things and I'm doing what I love, which is supervising the leisure activities. So, yes, it's busy. Bit different from when it was the health club! It's going to be busy every week until August. Then Jeremy and I are having a holiday.'

Suddenly everyone was arriving, among them Harriet. 'Had to come. Mother's sitting in for me. Hello, every-body.' She was greeted by a chorus of 'Hello, Harriet.'

'What have you done with Jimbo?' Venetia asked.

'He's in Bristol doing the VIP food at a big toy fair.'

Caroline came in from the kitchen carrying two coffee pots, which she put down beside the cups. She tapped a spoon loudly on the side of one of them. 'Right, ladies, I think we can begin. Please do come along and help yourselves, you'll be glad to hear we're not counting the calories tonight! Eat as much as you can! There's a dish on the gâteaux table and one where we're serving the coffee for your money. Muriel and Sylvia are in charge of the gâteaux and I'm serving coffee. Sheila Bissett, just back from her round the world trip, see how tanned she is, hardly recognised you Sheila, is in charge of the bring and buy. Enjoy!'

Muriel and Sylvia, stationed behind the table to serve the slices of gâteau, had a busy time. Muriel loved the delicate china plates and the silver cake forks and the delightful flowered napkins she folded and presented to each person as they took their plates. When she had a moment to spare between serving, she glanced round and thought how lovely the dining room looked. Caroline had put a crystal chandelier in place of the bulb dangling on the end of a piece of cable that Mr Furbank had had all those years. Lovely vases of flowers stood on any and every surface, and the carpet and the curtains had a slight oriental look which Muriel adored. If she'd married Mr Furbank, she'd have been stuck with a lifetime of dangling light bulbs. She blushed at her narrow escape. Well, not escape, because he'd never asked her and never would have done, but she had fancied him.

Georgie Fields came carrying her empty plate.

'More gâteau, Georgie?'

'Yes, the raspberry meringue this time, please, Lady Templeton.'

'Left Bryn in charge of the bar have you?'

'Yes. Couldn't miss this. The first elegant social "do" there's been since we got here.'

'Business doing well?'

'Oh yes. We were a bit apprehensive about moving out into the sticks as it were, we've always worked in towns before you see, but I must say it's been a complete success. Especially now with the dining room, that's really made us take off.' She placed a large piece of meringue in her mouth and, waving her cake fork at Sylvia, mumbled had she settled down to married life now?

'Yes, thank you, best day's work I ever did.'

'Wish I could get Alan married off. As a barman he's second to none, but at the moment he's sex mad. He can think of nothing else. I've told him, he'll find the right one eventually, but no, he's after anything in skirts. At thirty-two I expect he thinks it's time he got cracking.'

'You've known him a long time?'

'He's worked for us since he left school, he hasn't a family so it's good for him that he can live in. But I've told him, no girls on the premises, thank you. I won't have it.'

Pat Duckett overheard the conversation as she waited for Muriel to serve her a slice of the chocolate gâteau Venetia had brought.

'Nobody likes him, yer know,' she said. 'Good at his job but he's not liked.'

Georgie was upset. 'No one likes him? That's the first I've heard. Why ever not?'

'Slimy 'e is, slimy.' Muriel who agreed with Pat but didn't like to say so, muttered that 'perhaps that was a little unkind'.

'Unkind it might be, but it's the truth.' Pat thanked Muriel for the gâteau and, helping herself to another napkin, wandered off for what she hoped would be a worthwhile chat with Venetia.

Muriel did her best to pour oil on troubled waters. 'You'll have to excuse Pat, I'm afraid, she's very upset at the moment and doesn't know what she's saying.'

'Why?'

'Short of money and the children getting more expensive each year to feed and clothe, and now her father's coming to live with her, because he's just lost his job.'

'Oh dear, poor Pat. Yes, well, she does have problems, I suppose.'

'Yes, she does.' Muriel looked across the dining room to where she could see Pat talking to Venetia. They looked very intent.

'You see, my dad knows everything there is to know about gardening and then some. He's done it all his life. All he needs is a chance to prove it.'

'Well, I could ask Jeremy if he needs anyone.'

'He specialises in glasshouse work, but he can turn his 'and to anything actually.'

'You mean greenhouses?'

'Yes, he's been growing vines and peaches and figs and things all his working life. If it's under glass, you name it 'e grows it.'

'Look Pat, it's nothing to do with me, Jeremy's in charge of the estate, but I'll certainly have a word. I mean we never looked after the greenhouses when we owned it, and nothing's been done since Crad— Mr Fitch came, so yes, I do know they need attention. But then he's so forward looking. Cut your losses and start a new project, you know the kind of thing. He could quite easily say, pull the lot down, they're not worth the trouble. But I promise I'll see what I can do.'

'Thank you, yer've no idea what a help it would be if he got a job. I can't stand the thought of him round the house all day and nothing to do. I mean he was only nineteen when I was born so he's still got plenty of go in him. He's not ready for the scrap heap yet. More coffee? This one's on me.'

Harriet came to the table asking for another slice of raspberry meringue.

'I've no doubt I shall regret this around two o'clock this

morning and will be lying in bed munching indigestion tablets, but there you are.'

Sylvia handed her the meringue and a fresh napkin, and was about to ask Harriet if the children were excited about the baby when the uproarious arrival of a crowd from Penny Fawcett put paid to any further conversation they might have liked to have.

It was quite late when Caroline's guests began to leave. Muriel stayed behind to help clear up.

'What a wonderfully successful evening, Caroline. How much money have we made?'

'Believe it or believe it not, I've counted up and it's a hundred and eighty-five pounds, seventy-five pence. Isn't that marvellous? The bring and buy stall just helped to top it up and we had far more people than I expected. I couldn't believe it when the minibus from Penny Fawcett turned up. I knew some of them intended coming, but a minibus full! There were so many they were sitting on each others' knees. Good thing the sergeant didn't catch them!'

'Brilliant!' Harriet said. 'That's just a bit more than we needed to finish the refurbishment, isn't it? Now, I'm going to give a hand.'

'Oh no, you're not, you can be purely decorative, Harriet, and entertain us with dynamic conversation while we work. Muriel and I will clear up. There's not that much to do now. Pat did a lot for me before she left.' Caroline smiled at her as she bent over the dishwasher. 'Sit in my rocking chair and watch. I won't put this plate of yours in, Muriel, it might be the worse for wear if I do, we'll wash that in the sink.'

'By the way, Jimbo's asked Pat Duckett if she'd like some evening work waitressing when he has an outside catering job.' As she said this Harriet bent forward for a moment, and then continued. 'I know she would welcome the money and I'm sure she'd be relia— Gosh I've got the most incredible indigestion. I should never have eaten like I did. There's not enough room left any more for overeating. My insides can't cope. Hell, I don't know what can have made it so bad. Wow.'

'I've got some indigestion tablets, Harriet, would you like one?'

'Yes, please.' Caroline searched in a cupboard for them and eventually found the packet. Harriet took one gratefully. She sat quietly chewing the tablet and waiting for it to take effect.

'Would either of you like a drink before you go? Tea or something?' She turned to ask Harriet what she would like. 'Tea for you . . . Are you all right?'

'Things have improved I must say. It must be that meringue thing I had to finish with.'

Caroline said, 'Are you sure it's indigestion?'

'Yes. It must be, the tablet's eased it now. Where's Peter tonight?'

'Playing squash with an old college friend. He felt guilty, but I said it's a ladies' evening and we can manage perfectly well without you, so off you go.'

'It never ceases to amaze me that men think we can't cope without them. Jimbo was all hot under the collar before he left. You've got to go, I insist, I said . . . Oh dear, I've a nasty feeling it's not . . . indigestion.'

Caroline put her hand on Harriet's stomach and felt it harden as a contraction took hold. 'You're in labour.'

'Don't be ridiculous, Caroline, how can I be in labour, it simply isn't convenient at the moment with Jimbo away. I can't be, anyway it's three more weeks yet. I can't be. Can I?' She looked up at Caroline and as their eyes met they both acknowledged that she very likely was. 'Whatever will Jimbo say?'

'Have you a bag packed?'

'No. Didn't think I'd be needing it just yet. It's a false alarm. I'll go home and get to bed. Yes, that's it, I'm feeling odd because I've got overtired and I've got this blessed indigestion.'

Caroline suggested an ambulance might be more appropriate. 'Let's time two more contractions, and then we'll make our decision. Tell me when the next one starts. You watch the clock, Muriel.' Neither Caroline nor Harriet noticed the look on Muriel's face. If they had they would have got her a chair to sit on before she fell down.

Caroline saw a look of concentration come into Harriet's face. 'Now, Muriel.'

'It's ten past ten.'

'Right. Let's wait for the next one. Sit down, Muriel, it may be some time.'

They waited only eight minutes before the next contraction came.

'Shouldn't I be doing something, like boiling a kettle?' Her faint squeaky voice made Caroline look at her.

'Do you know what, I think it would be a good idea if you went across to Henderson's and got Sadie to pack a bag for Harriet. Could you do that now?'

'Of course, you don't need the kettle then?'

'If you like.' Muriel filled it, put it on the Aga and then quietly let herself out into the dark street. She scurried down Stocks Row and past The Royal Oak, where everyone appeared to be behaving quite normally, a fact which Muriel found difficult to understand in the circumstances.

She hammered on the front door of Henderson's and

strained to hear Sadie coming down the hall. 'Come on, Sadie, come on.'

The door opened sharply. Sadie peered out into the dark. 'Heavens! Muriel! Is there a fire?'

'Fire? Oh no, it's Harriet. She's – she's gone into labour and it's very quick and Caroline said could you get her a bag ready for the hospital and she's thinking she will have to ring for the ambulance. Oh Sadie, I don't know anything about these things but it does seem to me that it's nearly here. Harriet is in such great pain, I don't know how she can bear it.'

'Oh my God, come in. Oh dear. I'm much too old for this kind of thing, I did tell her not to do it, but she never listens to me.' Sadie fluttered about the hall distractedly, still managing to look elegant despite her anxiety. 'Wait here, I'll run upstairs and see what I can find.'

Muriel waited on the hall chair, restless to be off, but at the same time wishing she didn't need to return to the rectory. She couldn't leave Caroline to cope on her own, could she? She had to be brave and stick it out. Before Ralph came, life was so quiet and untroubled and now it seemed as though at every turn she was facing challenge. She heard Sadie opening and shutting drawers upstairs, then heard her collecting bottles and things in the bathroom. Then footsteps on the landing and Sadie came hurrying down, bag in hand.

'Give her my love and tell her I'll hold the fort till Jimbo gets back tomorrow. Oh God, I shall have to phone him on his mobile. He'll go mad. Tell her I'll stay here all night, OK?'

Muriel fled as fast as she could back to the rectory hampered by the weight of the bag. Surely Harriet wouldn't need all this stuff? Anyone would think she was going in for a month.

Caroline opened the door. 'I've rung for the ambulance, it won't be long now.' Muriel handed her the bag and hesitatingly re-entered the kitchen. Harriet was standing up holding on to the edge of the kitchen table, her back bent, her whole body concentrating on managing the pain.

In a brief respite between the pains Harriet said, 'Terribly sorry about this. It's nearly here, you know.'

'I know it is.' They all three heard the ambulance draw up outside and Muriel fled to open the door.

The ambulance men came in to the kitchen and shook hands with Caroline as though they had all the time in the world.

'Well now, nice to see you back in harness again, Doctor. We've got here as quickly as we could. You were in good hands, Mrs Charter-Plackett, well known for being cool in a crisis is our Dr Harris.'

The telephone rang and Muriel went to answer it.

'The Rectory here.'

'Who's that?'

'Muriel Hipkin . . . oh, no, I mean Templeton. Oh dear.'

'Jimbo Charter-Plackett here. I've had a phone call about Harriet. Sadie gave a very incoherent message to one of my assistants, and I can't understand it. They said I'd to ring the rectory.'

'Well Jimbo, Harriet can't come to the phone at the moment, because the ambulance has just arrived and she's going to hospital as quickly as possible because Caroline says the baby is nearly here.'

'Oh my God. Oh my God. Is she all right?'

'Yes, she's doing fine.'

'Oh my God, oh my God. What shall I do? I knew I

shouldn't have left her. I did tell her. I don't believe it. It's so early.'

'She's made a kind of grand finale to the Coffee Evening.'

'Tell Harriet I love her and I'm coming home as soon as I've rearranged things for tomorrow.'

'Jimbo don't come home, go directly to the hospital.'

'Of course, of course, I'm not thinking straight. Thank Caroline for me, please.'

Muriel started to say, 'Drive carefully', but the phone went dead so she replaced the receiver.

When she returned to the kitchen the ambulance men had wrapped Harriet in a blanket and were about to get her into the ambulance. 'Harriet, my dear, that was Jimbo. He sends his love and he's going directly to the hospital.'

Caroline followed them out of the door and laid Harriet's holdall on the floor of the ambulance. 'Good luck. It won't be long now. I'll ring in an hour and see how you are.' When Harriet had gone, Caroline went back into the rectory to thank Muriel for her help and to make a cup of tea she'd promised when they were clearing up.

Muriel was sitting ashen-faced on a kitchen chair, her forearms resting in the table.

'I know I must look awful, I'm so sorry, but I'm not used to babies coming and it's upset me a great deal. I thought it was going to come here in the kitchen.'

'So did I. Thank heavens they got here quickly. I'm shattered. It's a long time since I did maternity.'

'I'm going home now to have a cup of camomile tea to steady my nerves. Thank you for a lovely evening, Caroline. I'm so glad it was such a success. Harriet will be all right, won't she?'

'Of course, don't worry. Babies do come quickly sometimes.'

Chapter 11

Flick sat on the front pew swinging her legs, having a word with God. 'Thank you God for sending me a little sister. All this time I thought we were getting a boy. I really needed a girl. It's hard being the only female, you know, and I didn't think you understood. I've chosen a name for her. I think she looks as if she needs a dignified name. I'm Felicity really, you see, but I couldn't say it when I was little and it turned into Flick, so I've thought and thought and I think I'd like to call her Frances Charlotte Charter-Plackett. What do you think?'

She screwed up her eyes very tightly and waited for His reply. She hoped He was listening; after all, she was being naughty not going to school when Daddy thought she was there. But there are days when you can't do what you ought, and it's not every day a girl gets a new sister. 'It will have to begin with F, you see, or she'll think she doesn't belong to Finlay and Fergus and me, and I wouldn't want her to think she's adopted. She is beautiful, God, and I want to thank you for being so kind as to send me a pretty sister. I wouldn't have wanted an ugly one. But I do think you let Mummy leave it a bit late. It's not funny being born in an ambulance in the hospital car park. Whatever will she think when she grows up? She'll think we've been careless. When we get Mummy home tomorrow I shall tell her, Frances Charter-Plackett. It sounds very distinguished, don't you think?'

Flick heard footsteps, so she opened her eyes. It was Peter coming out of the choir vestry.

'Hello, Flick. Isn't it wonderful news about your new sister?'

'Hello, Mr Harris. Yes, but I wish you'd sent for me, I've been reading all about it, I could have helped.'

'Your sister was in the most tremendous hurry, I don't think Mrs Harris had time to think about sending for help.'

'She is a proper doctor, isn't she? You called her Mrs Harris then.'

'Well, yes, she is. I should have said Dr Harris in the circumstances, I know.'

'I'm so glad I've got a little sister. When you see her you'll think she's very beautiful, you know. Just as beautiful as your Beth.'

Willie came in through the church door, wearing his gardening clothes. 'Oh, there you are Flick, your Dad's out of his mind. They've just rung from the school to say you never arrived. He's been out looking for you. He's gone back to the Store now, 'cos they're so busy this morning with everyone wanting to hear about your new baby.'

'I'd better go, then. He panics you know, Mummy says he does anyway. He does need me to look after him with her away. Bye bye.' Flick went out into the rain, her pigtails flapping as she ran.

Willie chuckled. 'A right old-fashioned little girl she is, and no mistake. Anyways, sir, I know it's raining but I'm going to make a start on extending that brick path by the . . . ' He stopped speaking, halted by the sound of the most horrendous crash. He and Peter looked at each other, fear in their eyes. Without a word Peter picked up the skirts of his cassock and raced out through the door and down the path with Willie close behind, the rain lashing at them as they ran.

They found Flick lying misshapenly, face down in the middle of the road just past the lych gate, blood slowly seeping from her head onto the tarmac. The car which had run her down was slammed against the churchyard wall beyond the lych gate, with Alan Crimble still in the driver's seat, his head resting on the steering wheel. He too had blood seeping from his head, running in dribbles onto his knees. The silence was harrowing.

Willie went to turn Flick over. Peter shouted urgently, 'Don't move her. Get Caroline. Ring for an ambulance. Quick.' He knelt down in the road beside Flick and listened for her breathing. Shock. Yes, shock. Keep her warm. He unbuttoned his cassock and laid it over her. There were footsteps and it was Jimbo and then suddenly a crowd. Jimbo knelt on the road beside Flick. Deathly white, breathing as though he'd run in a race. His head almost touching the road, he looked into her face for signs of life. Almost afraid to touch her, he gently laid the back of his hand on her cheek. He pulled Peter's cassock more closely around her shoulders. Tucked it carefully around her small bare feet. He looked up at Peter. Inside themselves they both wept.

Peter went to attend to Alan. He sat motionless, crouched over the wheel. The windscreen had shattered and the crazed glass cast curious broken light on Alan's head. The blood still drip-dripping on to his trousers. Peter managed to force the car door open. He touched Alan's shoulder. Slowly his head came up. Peter saw a great gash on his forehead. Instinctively, he got a freshly laundered handkerchief from his trouser pocket and gave it to Alan to press to his head.

Peter helped him to get out of the car. Alan moved as though in a trance. He straightened up. He was dreadfully sick right there on the road. Peter turned away. He could see Caroline kneeling beside Flick. Jimbo was beside her, his hand on Caroline's shoulder. Waiting. Waiting.

'I can feel her pulse, Jimbo. All we can do is keep her warm until the ambulance arrives. They won't be long.'

Jimbo cleared his throat and tried to speak but the words wouldn't come. He gestured with his hands helplessly. Caroline patted his arm and smiled reassuringly. She stayed kneeling on the road beside Flick, stroking her hair and talking to her. The crowd, now much larger but still silent, stood watching Alan Crimble leaning against the church wall, handkerchief to his head, deathly white and panting.

Jimbo noticed him for the first time and in a flash galvanised himself into action. His voice, dry and choking, pushed its way out of his throat. 'I'll kill you for this.' In a moment he was across the road and his hands were around Alan's throat, squeezing, squeezing.

Peter grabbed Jimbo's wrists and forced his hands away from Alan's neck. Peter spoke firmly. 'This won't do Jimbo, go talk to Flick, she needs you. I'll take care of Alan.'

Alan found his voice; a small, thin piping voice begging for understanding.

'I never saw her, she came out of the gate and I'd hit her before I could do anything. I couldn't help it, it wasn't my fault she ran into the road without looking. I really couldn't help it. They can't blame me. They can't.'

'Compose yourself, Alan. Jimbo's very overwrought,

you'll have to excuse him.'

'Is she . . . you know, is she dead?'

'No.'

'Thank God.'

'But she's badly hurt.'

Caroline left Jimbo to comfort Flick and went to speak to Alan. She lifted Peter's handkerchief from his forehead and examined the gash.

'You'll be needing stiches, Alan, but not to worry, it doesn't look too serious. How do you feel everywhere else?'

'All right I think, but I feel so cold.' He was trembling from head to foot.

Caroline looked at the silent crowd. They were standing completely still showing no emotion.

'Anyone a coat they could lend Alan? It's the shock, he's feeling cold.'

The question stirred them.

'So he should be.'

'Serves 'im right.'

'So?'

They began a kind of ugly murmuring which left to itself could have become explosive. Peter said in a loud voice, 'I have a blanket in my car, use that.' He gave Caroline the keys. She left him to face the crowd. His height gave him the advantage. Peter deliberately caught their eyes to stare them down. One by one they looked at him and then, outstared, glanced shamefacedly down.

'Flick will need all our prayers and love. And so will Alan, he didn't deliberately run her down, it was an accident.'

The sound of the ambulance siren could be heard as it came down the Culworth Road. The crew jumped out almost the moment it pulled up. Peter felt as though they had taken at least an hour to arrive, but when he checked his watch he found scarcely fifteen minutes had passed since he'd first heard the noise of the crash.

Caroline suggested Jimbo should go in the ambulance. He held her arm. 'Yes, yes, of course.' He pleaded with her for advice. 'Caroline, how am I going to tell Harriet?'

'Very, very gently, and with hope, Jimbo.'

The ambulance man nodded in the direction of Alan Crimble. 'We'll take this gentleman too, Dr Harris.'

'Of course. It looks like he only has that head wound, but he's in shock.'

He turned aside and said quietly to Caroline, 'You don't need me to tell you the little girl's in a bad way, Doctor.'

'I know, I know.'

'Very bad, actually.'

The driver stood waiting to close the ambulance doors. Alan, still wrapped in Peter's blanket, climbed unsteadily up the steps. Jimbo followed him in. The other ambulance man was inside attending to Flick, who lay on the stretcher silent and still, so contrary to the way she lived her life. The driver slammed the doors shut and strode round to the front to climb in the cab. He acknowledged Caroline's wave and then drove steadily out of the village. The crowd, left behind with no one to vent their anger on, drifted away in twos and threes, talking quietly.

Caroline pulled herself together to face the realities. 'I'm going to the Store, Peter, do you think we should close it for the rest of the day?'

'With both Harriet and Jimbo not there, I think there's no alternative. I'll come with you.' Caroline saw Flick's blue flip-flops by the churchyard wall; rather strangely they were laid side by side, as if Flick had taken them off and put them neatly there to await her return. She carried them across to the Store, tears welling in her eyes. They looked so forlorn there in her hand, as though they felt of no use any more.

When they got into the Store, Sadie was behind the counter, tears pouring down her face. 'I'm not brave, I couldn't go out to see her.' She asked Caroline what she thought. 'What do you think? She isn't dead is she?'

'No, she isn't, but it is very serious. There are several bones broken. But I know the orthopaedic surgeon, Archie McKintyre, he's an outstanding man. If anyone can do anything for her, he will. He is quite brilliant. Very innovative.' Caroline put her arm round Sadie and hugged her tight.

'I'm being a damned old fool. For the boys' sakes I shall have to pull myself together.'

'What about closing the Store? You can't cope with everything and the boys will need your support, they can't be left alone.'

'How sensible. Linda write me a notice, "Shop closed temporarily, sorry for any inconvenience." If they complain they know what they can do. Tomorrow I shall get organised and bring in some help. Pray for her Peter, I'm sure your prayers will count for more than mine.'

Peter smiled gently. 'I don't believe that for one minute.'

Caroline held out Flick's flip-flops. 'I found these in the road.' Sadie cradled them against her face, and whispered 'God help us all.'

At midday Caroline rang the hospital for news. She went to tell Peter in his study. 'They're taking her into theatre right now. Fractured skull, and several broken bones including both legs and her pelvis. But she's holding her own very well. She's a tough little girl, with lots of determination, if anyone can pull through she will.'

'Poor Harriet. At such a vulnerable time too. I think I'll be off to the hospital. God knows what you say to parents at this moment.'

'I know you'll find the right words, you always do.' She kissed him and went to hug her own two children, playing with water in the kitchen sink while Sylvia made the lunch.

That night, without Alan, Bryn and Georgie were short-handed in the bar. Of course they were extremely busy: all their regulars had come in wanting to know what had happened and to pass their own verdict on where the blame lay.

'Told Alan more than once he should have his car serviced. Right mess it was, yer know, Bryn. Wrecker's yard out Penny Fawcett way was the best place for it. That's where it will end up now, and not before time. You should've insisted.'

Bryn stroked his big moustache and replied, 'I'm not his keeper, only his employer.'

'Yer could have advised him.'

Bryn protested. 'He's a grown man and . . . '

'Grown man? He's a kid really. Irresponsible, that's what. Drives far too fast as we all know. See'd him once coming home from Culworth like a bat out of hell, however he made that sharp right hand turn by the signpost I'll never know. 'Nother time 'e scared the living daylights out of a friend of mine coming over that crossroads where the rector had his accident. Maniac behind a wheel, is Alan.'

'Police'll throw the book at him.' The speaker enumerated on his fingers the crimes of which he guessed Alan was guilty. 'Careless driving for a start. Driving without insurance. Driving without a road fund licence. No MOT. Tyres not up to snuff. Lights not working properly, and brakes not up to scratch, and that's *without* examining the car.'

Another regular pronounced in a loud voice, 'What's more I shan't want him serving me in 'ere of a night. Not a fella who can run a little girl down, and a lovely little girl she is too.'

Georgie, who'd kept silent until now, spoke up. 'Now look here, we all know that Flick ran out of the gate and into the road without looking, and Alan didn't see her because of the lych gate. She came straight out at him, he'd no time.'

'Even if he had had time to see her he couldn't have stopped because his brakes weren't good enough. If you'll take my advice you'll give him the order of the boot.'

'The order of what?'

'Give him his cards, finish him, sack him or whatever they call it nowadays. When will he be out of hospital?'

'Tomorrow, most likely.'

'Well, give him his notice tomorrow then.'

'I shall do nothing of the sort. Tell him that the day he comes out? That's not very Christian, is it? We've no cause to do that, he's a good worker, knows this business like the back of his hand. In any case Bryn and I employ whom we wish in our pub, it is our business after all.'

'It is, you're absolutely right and it's a free world. But if yer want yer takings to slump, you keep him.' Bryn quietly shook his head at Georgie, whose temper was beginning to boil up, and she let the matter go. The customers took their drinks to a table and left the two of them battling to keep everyone served.

It was two days after her operation before Flick regained

consciousness. Harriet, shocked beyond endurance by the news of the accident, had been kept in hospital; she was taken in a wheelchair to the orthopaedic ward, where she sat in Flick's side ward watching and waiting. She couldn't bear seeing the tubes and the machines surrounding Flick. She couldn't tolerate the twenty-four-hour attention from the nurses, it seemed Flick was never left in peace. She almost begged them to leave her alone and let her go. Then she persuaded herself that while there was life there was hope. Jimbo, kept better informed than Harriet, didn't dare sound too encouraging.

They were both there when Flick opened her eyes. She gave the tiniest smile when she saw Jimbo and Harriet leaning over her.

'Darling, it's Mummy. Daddy's here too.'

'Frances, where's Frances?' Her eyes closed, and she drifted away again.

To cover his relief Jimbo said impatiently, 'What's she talking about? Who's Frances? Is it someone at school?'

'It's not anyone at school. I've never heard her mention Frances. I haven't the faintest idea. But Jimbo, she's coming round. She spoke, so that must be a good sign surely, Sister?'

'It certainly is, it certainly is. Still a long road to travel, but that's very positive.'

Jimbo became possessed with an idea. 'Sister, do you think it would be a good move if we brought the baby down from the maternity ward and let her see her? It might just trigger her into staying awake, mightn't it?'

'What a good idea. I'll phone Sister in maternity and ask how she feels about it. We could keep her here until Flick wakes again, couldn't we? The staff will be delighted. They'll all be in to see her.'

When Flick opened her eyes again, Jimbo lifted the baby from her cradle and held her where Flick could see her.

'Look darling, look who's come to see you. Flick, look Flick.'

He held the baby close to Flick's face and waited for her response.

Flick smiled, and in a tiny voice said, 'Hello, Frances,' and then drifted away again.

'Harriet, she wants to call the baby Frances, that's what it is, she wants to call her Frances. Well, we shall if it pleases her. Frances. I like that.'

'So do I. She's beginning to come round, isn't she, Sister?'

'It's encouraging anyway, I must say. Now you must both go and wait outside. Mr McKintyre is on his way.'

After the surgeon had examined Flick, he spoke with Jimbo and Harriet, waiting out in the corridor. 'Not out of the woods yet, but I must say the wee one's holding her own. A little fighter she is, yes, a little fighter. Early days, early days, but you'll be pleased to know the word "hope" has entered our vocabulary. Lovely wee bairn you've got there, Mrs Charter-Plackett. See you again.'

Chapter 12

With the morning's post came a letter from Ralph's solicitor confirming his absolute right to the ownership of the spare land. 'At last we can go ahead, Muriel, my dear. Look, read this.' After she'd read it she asked, 'But Ralph, how did it all come about? Why should the spare land be yours again after all these years? Who made the mistake?'

'First things first. My great-great-great-grandfather Tristan Templeton, who lived at the end of the eighteenth century, was a racing man, and a gambler. Fortunately, he usually won so he didn't devastate the family fortunes. He had a rival Geoffrey de Guillet, living in the old manor house in Little Derehams. All that's left of it are the walls of the old kitchen garden which the council have turned into the rose garden. You know which one I mean?'

Muriel nodded. 'Well, his rival threw out a challenge that he could beat my great-great-great-grandfather Tristan in any race he cared to suggest. They decided on a race starting at the stocks here in Turnham Malpas and finishing at the market cross in Culworth. The wager was that if Tristan won he would get the spare land as his prize, something he had always coveted. If Geoffrey de Guillet won he would get Tristan's prize racehorse. Well, Tristan Templeton won the race by three lengths. The deeds for the land were duly handed over. All the rest of the estate was in one large piece. The spare land he'd won was quite separate from it. When the council bought the estate in 1946 they intended using Home Farm and the surrounding woods and fields for teaching the orphan boys farming skills so they could earn a living when they left the home. All that didn't work out and the council sold off the estate except for that piece immediately surrounding the Big House and Sykes Wood.'

'Which is the land still belonging to the Big House?'

'Quite right. The council *assumed* the spare land belonged to them, but due to a slip-up in the original sales contract written in 1946 the land was not mentioned at all, but no one noticed that. I still have the deeds and this letter confirms officially that I have owned it all these years.'

'Well, isn't that amazing?'

'So now I can go ahead and see about building the houses.'

'I wouldn't wish to pry into your business affairs, Ralph, but how can you afford the money to build all these houses? Are you so well off?'

'No, my dear, are *we* so well off? We share everything.'

'Everything?'

'Yes. When we married I transferred half of everything I own to you.'

'To me? Was that what all those papers that I signed were about?'

'Yes, my dear.'

Muriel was aghast. 'But I didn't give anything to you! I still have my money, well my bit of money in my own bank account. When you said about being "truly married" I thought you meant . . . you know . . . making love.'

'I did, but I meant money and possessions too.'

Hands clasped together under her chin, Muriel contemplated what Ralph had said. 'What a wonderful gesture. What a completely wonderful thing to have done. You make me feel very humble, dear, very humble. I don't really deserve your generosity. I just do not. I was so confused at the time when I signed those papers I simply didn't realise. You must have thought me very ungrateful.'

'Well, now you know.'

'So in that case I own half the spare land?'

Ralph thought for a moment and saw he was in a tight corner. 'Because we've only just discovered the spare land is mine – ours, on paper nothing is official. But yes, in theory you do.'

'I see. I'll go make the lunch.' She left Ralph contemplating what would be churning around in her mind while she made it. After a few minutes Muriel popped her head round the door and said, 'So, if you shared everything equally with me when we married, I can have a say in what we do about building the houses?'

Ralph hesitated and then said, 'Yes, of course. But I would expect you would heed my advice.'

'I see.' Muriel returned to the kitchen to finish the lunch.

Part way through eating her lunch, Muriel said, 'But, Ralph, I still have my own bank account with my small savings in and with the money in it from selling my cottage. I shall go to the bank this afternoon and transfer it all into . . . What shall I transfer it into?'

'Don't do it.' With a twinkle in his eye he said, 'If I lose all our money on this house caper, we might need yours to live on.'

Muriel was shocked. 'You don't mean that, do you? There really isn't very much, you know.'

'No, I was teasing. But don't transfer it, I rather like the idea of being married to a woman with money. Anyway it helps you to keep your independence.'

'I shall have a flutter on the Stock Exchange, Yes, that's what I shall do.'

'You're getting very daring, my dear.'

'No doubt I shall change my mind as soon as I've done it, but I've decided I fancy the idea of living dangerously. Oh, I do wish there was good news about Flick. That poor dear little girl. She's taken a turn for the worse because of the anaesthetic, and her lungs are affected now. She was, I mean *is*, such a joy. Jimbo is a shadow of what he used to be.'

'Look, she's held on for a week, she's conscious and she's talking lucidly, so there must be hope. She's a tough little thing, you know, really tough. If anyone can pull through she can. I saw that Alan Crimble this morning. Like Jimbo, he's a shadow of what he used to be too.'

'Oh dear. What's that expression they use about ice cream? I know, he won't be flavour of the month, will he?'

'No, it could be very distressing for him. But she did run out of the shadow of the lych gate and into the road, apparently without looking. So it's not entirely his fault. The police took his car away. I doubt they'll find it roadworthy.'

'He'll be prosecuted then?'

'Without a doubt. I have letters to write, Muriel. The lunch was lovely. I'll study the *Financial Times* if you like, and we'll choose some shares.'

'Thank you, dear. When I've cleared up I'm going to the Store for a card to send to Flick.'

Harriet went in to say *au revoir* to Flick before she left the hospital with the baby. She thought perhaps there wasn't quite so much machinery around her now, but she still looked like something from outer space.

'Flick, darling, it's Mummy. Hello-o-o, anyone at ho-o-ome?' Flick stirred, opened her eyes and said, 'Are you going now?'

'Yes, darling, I am. Daddy or I will be here every day to see you. But I've got to go now. I wasn't supposed to be here all this time in the first place, so I've outstayed my welcome. And the boys are needing me, too. Look, nurse has brought Frances up for you to see to say bye bye.'

'Bye bye Frances. Isn't she beautiful, Mummy? So beautiful. Take care of them all, Frances, till I get back.' Harriet held the baby close to Flick's face and she kissed her. 'We belong together, Fran and me, you know. We're *sisters*.' Flick closed her eyes, twinkled her fingers at them both and went to sleep. Harriet stood watching her. How close they'd come to losing her. How very close. That first terrifying night Harriet had become obsessed with the idea that she'd been given Frances in exchange for Flick, and that Flick would die. But thank the Lord, here they both were, and Flick improving a little every day. She'd make a rota and get her mother and anyone she possibly could to come to spend time with Flick. The next few weeks were going to be horrendous, but they'd win through, oh yes. For a brief moment Harriet thought about Alan Crimble. Damn him and his stupid car. She didn't think she could ever speak to him again.

Chapter 13

The problem of what to do about Alan was weighing heavily on the minds of Bryn and Georgie. Since Flick's accident things had been very uncomfortable for him. Despite Georgie's loyalty, Bryn and she were beginning to think that it would be better if they tactfully suggested Alan found another job.

There were some customers who refused point blank to be served by him; indeed some had walked out rather than have him pull their pints. The drop in takings was noticeable but not worrying. They dreaded the day his case would come up in court. It was very quiet in The Royal Oak this particular Saturday evening. The school parents were holding a Summer Barn Dance in the school hall, and there was the final whist drive of the summer season in the church hall. If their past experience was anything to go by, there would be a sudden influx of people shortly, all wanting to be served at the same time. Sure enough in they came, plus a group of young men holding a celebratory drink for a friend's twenty-first.

'Pint of bitter please, Bryn, what will you all have?' They sorted out what they wanted and while they waited for

Bryn to serve them, they were laughing and jostling each other. One of them spotted Alan.

'Hallo, Alan. Still 'ere then? Thought you'd have been gone long since. When does yer case come up?'

Alan smiled his thin, ingratiating smile. 'Too soon for me to know that. I may not even get prosecuted.'

'They'll throw the book at yer, and it's only what you deserve.'

Georgie spoke up. 'It wasn't entirely Alan's fault, you know, Flick did run out without looking.'

'We know that, but he still deserves whatever he gets. That car was a heap and no one in their right mind should have been driving it. Just thank yer lucky stars, Alan, she's still alive.' The young man, a redhead, picked up his drink and made to move to a table. 'Yer deserve a horse whipping, but I reckon you'll most likely get the easy option and go to prison.'

Alan shrank back against the optics. 'Think so?'

'More than likely.' Alan's tormentor grinned at his obvious distress, raised his glass in salute and joined his friends.

The bar began to fill up, so Alan had to go round the tables clearing away the used glasses and wiping away spills.

'By Jove, Bryn, Alan isn't a patch on Sharon MacDonald, we all enjoyed her backside slipping between the tables as she cleared away the glasses. Always ready for a bit of slap and tickle was Sharon. He's a poor substitute is Alan. We can't enjoy a glimpse of his cleavage!'

'It was more than a glimpse with Sharon.'

'Good for trade she was, though. Alan puts us off, don't yer, Alan?' The speaker gripped his shoulder. 'Heaven alone knows what he gets up to in that cellar, down there in the chill cold air, attending the beer. Got some pin-ups down there, Alan, to warm you up? See'd you Thursday at The Force. Right little raver yer were with. All backside and big ti . . . teeth. She yer latest then?'

Alan withstood this barrage as best he could, but Bryn could feel trouble brewing. Customers had been awkward and truculent with him since the accident but tonight there was a different feel about the joking. From behind the bar Bryn called out, 'Alan, we need some more bitter lemons and tonics, please.'

'Rightio, governor.'

'He'll be saying that in prison, 'cept it'll be "Certainly governor, yes sir, no sir, three bags full sir".' They laughed uproariously and began telling prison jokes.

Alan came back into the bar carrying the bottles Bryn had asked for. The twenty-first birthday crowd was getting noisier. One of them noticed Alan was back.

'You got any good jokes to tell us, Alan?'

The door swung open and in came Peter with the chairman of the school governors, his wife and Michael Palmer.

Peter called out, 'Good evening, everyone.' A chorus of 'Good evening, Rector,' came from the customers.

Peter took out his wallet and bought drinks for the four of them. They took them to the only spare table, and when they were satisfactorily seated Peter said, 'A toast to a very successful evening.' They echoed his words, and Michael said, 'And can I add a big thank you for all your support. I think it's been the best ever.'

Peter said, 'Most definitely.'

'I'm a great believer in school parents getting to know each other at social events. It all helps to pull them together as a team. I know of a village where . . . ' The chairman of the governers looked set for a big speech. His wife, reading the signals, decided to escape. She interrupted with, 'Excuse me, while I go to the little room.' Peter stood up as she rose from the table. Standing up gave him a good view of what was happening to Alan. He could see him clearing away glasses at the table where his tormentors were seated, then saw him unbalanced by a savage kick at his ankle. Alan clutched at the table to recover himself. 'Oh, whoops, he's had one over the eight, he's been indulging down in that cellar. We all wondered what he got up to down there, and now we know.'

'Come on, Alan, we'll buy you a drink to top you up. Double whisky for Alan, please, Bryn!'

'My bar staff don't drink when on duty, sorry.'

'This one does.' Two of them grabbed Alan and pinned his arms behind his back. The red-haired assailant picked up someone's whisky and began trying to force it down Alan's throat.

Peter glanced across at Bryn. He saw him nod meaningfully at Georgie, who disappeared straight away, and then Bryn came out from behind the bar.

'This is getting out of hand gentlemen, please. I won't have this.' Bryn spoke firmly.

'No, you won't, Alan is. Come on you demon driver, open yer mouth, that's it, that's it, that's the way, down the hatch.' The whisky was partly going down Alan's throat and partly running down his chin and splashing onto his shirt. Bryn stepped up and tried to pull one of the men away, but the others, enjoying the spectacle, dragged him off.

Peter walked purposefully towards Bryn, intending to give him moral support. The ugly situation was made worse by the fact that customers not directly involved were quite liking the idea of Alan getting some punishment. They all knew how long Flick had been in hospital and what a narrow escape she'd had, and they quite relished the thought that if the courts didn't punish him as he deserved, they certainly would.

Michael joined Peter and whispered, 'You grab the red-haired one, I'll get the other.'

Peter nodded. They both dived together, grabbing the two men from behind, and pulling their arms behind their backs. Neither of Alan's attackers had seen who'd pulled them away, all they knew was that the fun was at an end. As soon as Peter released his grip on his arms, the red-haired one spun himself round and without really looking at his victim swung his fist at Peter's jaw. Fortunately Peter's height lessened the impact, but even so he staggered.

Deathly silence. The customers froze. Georgie gasped. Bryn was rooted to the floor. Peter, determined to maintain control so his attacker wouldn't gain any satisfaction from what he'd done, stood steadily looking at his assailant.

One of the men pushed back his chair and stood up. 'Please, Rector, accept our apologies.'

'Apologies!' shouted Bryn. 'Going down on your knees and begging for mercy wouldn't be enough for what you've done tonight. The lot of you are banned. Banned, do you hear? Punching the rector! Causing mayhem in my bar! The courts will decide what happens to Alan, not a bunch of rabblerousers like you lot. And the court will decide what to do with you lot, too. Because when the police get here I shall tell them exactly what's happened. Then they'll throw the book at you.'

'We didn't mean any harm. Things got a bit out of hand.'

'Out of hand? I should say!'

'You shouldn't employ him in here.'

'Who I employ is my affair, not yours.'

'Well, if that's how you want it so be it, but we shan't want to drink in here.'

'I don't want you to drink here, and when the police . . .'

As though on cue the swing doors opened and in came the sergeant. He bent down to remove his bicycle clips and said, 'Now then, what have we here? My word, Rector, I could almost think someone had been giving you a good thumping.' The sergeant pretended to examine Peter's jaw. 'Now, who did that, I wonder? Ah, I see, don't need to look any further, you're the same lot I turned out of the Jug and Bottle in Penny Fawcett three weeks ago. Well, this time I'm definitely charging you.'

Peter started trying to speak in their defence, but the sergeant held up his hand and silenced him.

'No, Rector, I'm not listening to any excuses, sorry, but they need sorting. If I listen to you, sir . . . ' Two of the men were trying to slip away. ''Ere you two, not another step, stay right where you are.' The sergeant pointed with the end of his pen. 'Right there. If I listen to you, sir, I shall be buying them a drink and tucking them up in their beds with a goodnight kiss before the night's out. No, sir, this is it. They've met their Waterloo.' His ballpoint pen wouldn't write, so he licked the end of it to make it work and began writing in his black notebook.

Chapter 14

'Caroline, where are you?'

'In the nursery, Peter.'

He appeared in the doorway. 'I'm going to look a complete idiot in church this morning with this big bruise. It would be the very day we'll be using the altar silver for the first time and the church will be full. Is there anything I can do, do you think?'

Caroline traced her finger along his jawline and made him wince. 'Oh sorry, I didn't mean to hurt. It's swollen too, that ice we used last night didn't have the desired effect, did it? There won't be many rectors conducting matins this morning with a swollen jaw got in a pub brawl.'

'It wasn't a brawl, darling. Well, yes it was, but I wasn't part of it.' Alex flung his arms round Peter's legs and squeezed hard. 'No, no, Alex, this cassock's clean on, I don't want your sticky fingers on it, young man. Good boy. Well, what's the answer? It's no laughing matter.' Despite himself Peter had to laugh when he looked in the nursery mirror. Alex, whose vocabulary, though limited, was always spoken at the top of his voice, shouted, 'Dada poorly.' Beth looked on, thumb in mouth.

Caroline said, 'I hesitate to suggest this, but what about putting some makeup on to lessen the impact a bit?'

'Makeup? The congregation will have doubts about my sexual proclivities.'

Caroline grinned wickedly. 'I doubt it, with these two rampaging in the rectory pew! If I smooth moisturiser on I'll probably hurt you, so you do it and then put some powder on over the top.'

'No. I've decided, it's happened, everyone knows, so why worry. I'll go as I am.' He bent down to kiss her. She put her arms round his neck, laid her face against his good cheek, and whispered in his ear, 'Come, to think of it though, you do wear a skirt!'

Peter playfully slapped her bottom and escaped from the nursery with Caroline in pursuit. 'I'll see you later,' she shouted from half way down the stairs. The front door slammed and Caroline, laughing, captured Alex as he struggled down the stairs after his father.

'Nappy time you two, and then off to church.'

Mrs Peel, in the two years and a bit that Peter had been rector, had developed the music beyond her wildest dreams, Peter's educated interest and talent having inspired her to reach new heights. Caroline entered the church to find it filled with a haunting melody. No one chattered, they were all listening. The music set the mood wonderfully, and she felt grateful that Peter had such a wonderful atmosphere created for him before he began his part of the worship.

In between coping with the twins' energies and wishing for about the hundredth time that there was a crèche for the little ones, Caroline took time to admire the altar. The old silver gleamed in the special lights Willie had fitted. Willie had decided that if they were to have it all on display then display it they would, and he'd spent a long time trying first one combination and then another until he'd got the effect just right. Muriel and Ralph came in and sat in their front pew. She glanced along her pew just in front of the lectern and smiled at the two of them. Alex called out 'Mooey. Mooey,' and waved to Muriel.

'Shhhhh.' Caroline put her finger to her lips but Alex simply smiled. Then Mrs Peel began the processional hymn, and Beth settled herself for a sleep, as she always did when Peter came in. He claimed that the first time Beth stayed awake for his sermon he would know he'd finally reached the height of his preaching powers. Alex saw Peter and shouted 'Dada, Dada.' Caroline's finger on his lips was far too late. She knew he made the congregation smile each time he said it, but privately she knew it upset Peter.

The service went beautifully and Caroline, despite the harassment of Alex wriggling about and trying to sing in all the wrong places, found it a deeply spiritual occasion. That was the lovely thing about Peter's services, so simple, so easy to understand his message, and yet so thought-provoking and moving. He stood on the altar steps waiting for the sidesmen to bring their individual collection plates to him. The collection plate came round and Alex put his twenty pence piece in and one for Beth, who was still asleep. Caroline put her envelope in and watched the sidesman take the plate to the other side of the aisle. He paused, for what seemed an eternity, and stood looking at Ralph, quite still, collection plate in hand. From where she sat Caroline could almost feel the sparks fly between the two of them. Then he deliberately moved to the next pew without passing the plate to him. Ralph, who had looked him straight in the eye when he'd hesitated with the plate, quietly put his collection back in his pocket. Muriel blushed to the roots of her hair, took out her handkerchief with a trembling hand and dabbed at her top lip and forehead. The entire congregation noticed what had happened, including Peter, whose face was like thunder.

Mrs Peel, watching in the organ mirror for when the collection plates arrived at the altar steps, stumbled with her notes and had to stop and begin the phrase again. Caroline suddenly found she could hardly see for the haze of embarrassment which had come down in front of her eyes. At that moment Alex slipped off the pew and fell head first with a resounding clatter onto the floor. His screams reverberated around the church. In her handbag Caroline found his dummy and, though she hated him sucking it in public, she rescued it from its plastic bag and popped it into his mouth. The howling stopped as though by magic, and Caroline busied herself rubbing his head and examining it for damage. She waited apprehensively to see what Peter would do.

The sidesmen came to stand before Peter, and waited for him to hold the huge silver dish ready to receive the collection. He looked down on them in silence. The congregation waited with bated breath. He replaced the dish on the altar and stepped forward down the steps. Looking straight at the sidesman who had so resolutely refused to do his duty by Ralph and Muriel, he reached out and took the plate from him. Then Peter went to Ralph and stood patiently waiting while he got his collection out again. Of course it had caught in his pocket and there was a moment when Ralph was struggling, Mrs Peel was running out of music because of the delay, and loud sucking noises could be heard from the rectory pew.

Peter returned to the altar steps, put the collection plate

on his dish, and then waited to receive the others. Loud mutterings could be heard all over the church.

Caroline was never more glad to reach the end of the service. Beth woke as Peter left the church. Caroline collected the two of them together and headed for the church porch to stand with Peter ready to shake hands with the congregation, but Peter was nowhere to be seen and she stood there by herself.

'So sorry, Dr Harris, whatever came over 'im?'

'What's it all about, do you know, Dr Harris?'

'Well, I never, what a to do. You all right then, little Alex, all right are yer? Rare old tumble you had there, and not half.'

'What with the rector's jaw and little Alex's head, good job you're a doctor, ain't it?'

'Your Beth's as good as gold in church, but little Alex is a right card.' The speaker patted their heads. 'We'll have to start a crèche, what with your two and little Frances now, and there's them from Nightingale Farm, right brood they've got up there and no mistake. Four it is now, and not one of 'em at school yet. They can't keep four of 'em quiet in the pew, can theys?'

'He needs telling off, he does. Hope the rector gives it him good and proper.'

In the vestry the sidesman *was* getting it good and proper.

'No matter what your views are in this matter, Arthur, the church is not the place to air them.'

'He's no right to be making money out of the villagers. He's got plenty and he needs no more than what he's got, he's not that many years left and no one to inherit.'

'Sir Ralph's financial status has absolutely nothing to do with this matter. You deliberately prevented him from offering himself to God's service. This is what one is doing when one puts money in the offertory. Giving oneself as well as the money.'

'Well, you would see it like that, Rector. It's my opinion the church doesn't want his kind of money. They say he's building a hundred houses on there. What hope have we for a real village life with that landed on us?'

'So providing homes for villagers which they can afford is a nonsense is it?'

'Not a nonsense, Rector, a money-making deal that's what it is. He'll get planning permission, sell the land to the highest bidder and pocket the money. Money, money, money, that's all he thinks about. Next news we'll have yobbos and drugs and joy riding, it'll never be the same again.'

'That could be a danger, and whilst I appreciate your views, you have no right whatsoever to do what you did this morning. None. Absolutely none. I am deeply grieved, Arthur, deeply grieved. It leaves me feeling very sad.'

'I'm deeply grieved too.'

'I get the feeling that there's more to this. Is there something I don't know, or is it just the houses?'

Arthur paused for a moment and then said, 'As you say, just the houses.' He stopped again, thought for a few seconds, and then taking a deep breath said: 'I object to him sitting in his Lord of the Manor pew, with his Lord of the Manor look on his face, making money hand over fist by spoiling our village. As if he's got some kind of supreme right to do as he wishes because of what he was. I'm not the only one who thinks like that either. T'ain't Christian.'

'That's a matter between Sir Ralph and his God. I'm afraid an apology is needed.'

'To you?'

'To me. Oh yes! And best of all to Sir Ralph.'

Arthur shook his head. 'Oh no, not to him. But I will apologise to you, Rector. I'm sorry for what I did this morning and if it caused you grief then, yes, I'm very sorry. But I shall be one of the people who gets up a petition, see if I don't. I can't stand by and let it happen without a protest.'

'Thank you for your apology and it's accepted whole-heartedly. Friends again, Arthur?' Peter held out his hand. 'And next Sunday?'

'I'll take the collection at the back not the front, there'll be no repetition of this morning, Rector, that I promise.' Arthur looked up at Peter and smiled. He shook Peter's hand vigorously. 'You've a very persuasive way with you, Rector. That wife of yours must have a devil of a job getting her own way about things. You could charm a monkey out of a tree, you could. Glad we've got you here at St Thomas's, though. You're the best thing that's happened in a long time. I'll say good morning to you. See you next Sunday.' As he left the vestry he turned at the door, smiled and said, 'Will you sign my petition?'

'I'll think about it!'

Peter went out in search of Ralph, but he and Muriel had already left.

'My dear Muriel, sit down here in your favourite chair and I'll make you a cup of tea, I think that's just what you need.' He disappeared into the kitchen. Muriel didn't like him in there, it didn't feel to be a man's job making tea, but at the moment she was grateful. In church, to be rebuffed in church like that. In front of everybody. She felt so mortified. That was what made it feel so bad. He'd shown them up in front of everyone. How could that Arthur Prior do it to them? What business was it of his, anyway? She'd dread the collection being taken every Sunday from now

133

on, wondering if he would do it again. People didn't care any more what they did or who they hurt, so long as they made their protest. She'd never dare show her face in church, not ever. How could she tell Ralph to abandon the idea of the houses, when he was so set on it?

He came in with the tray at that moment. 'I'll pour, you sit there and relax.' He sat with his hands resting on his knees, watching her and waiting for the tea to brew. 'Don't worry, my dear, it will all blow over. They'll all talk a lot and make a big fuss but we shall quietly get on with our project and they'll all come round, see if they don't. When they see how tastefully designed your houses are they'll love 'em.' She watched his elegant hands as they poured her tea, she never tired of watching them, so sensitive they were, really very artistic. When he placed her cup on the table beside her chair she said, 'Oh Ralph, I thought I was going to die.' Muriel took a sip of her tea. 'What a humiliation. I could strangle that Arthur. What right has he to sit in judgement on us? Peter was very upset.'

'He'd every right to be.'

'I shall never go to St Thomas's ever again. We'll have to go to church in Culworth.'

'Generations of the Templeton family have worshipped in St Thomas's. I've no intention of allowing Arthur to stop *me*, the very last of them.'

'We're both assuming it's about the spare land. I expect that *was* it, wasn't it?'

Ralph emphatically agreed. 'Yes.'

'Maybe we should forget the whole thing and leave it as it has always been, a lovely piece of nature for us all to enjoy. If Arthur comes round here to apologise I shall run upstairs out of the way. Say I'm indisposed or something.'

'Living dangerously hasn't lasted long.' Ralph smiled and patted her shoulder.

'I'm not very consistent, am I?'

The bell rang, and they heard the door opening. Muriel looked petrified, but then she heard Peter's voice.

'Hello there, Peter here, may I come in?' He appeared in the sitting-room doorway.

Ralph stood up. 'Come in, come in.'

'Come to offer my apologies about this morning in church. Arthur has apologised to me but he won't come here and apologise to you, Ralph. It's all about the spare land. He claims you are going to sell it with planning permission for a hundred houses. Is this true?'

'I am still waiting for confirmation from the council that they agree the land is definitely mine. When I've got that in writing from their solicitors, I shall apply for permission to build houses for rent on it. How many I do not know, as yet. That's the story Peter.'

'I see. Well, thanks for telling me. You all right, Muriel? Don't worry, it won't happen again, he's promised.'

'Are *you* all right, after the fight in the bar last night?'

'Yes, apart from my colourful bruise. You see, that's what Arthur is worried about, masses of houses and bringing in what he considers are all the wrong influences like brawling, drugs, motorbikes and that kind of thing.'

'Well, we'll see, we'll see.' Ralph stood up and Peter took the hint.

'I'll be on my way then. See you soon. I'll let myself out.'

When Peter had closed the door, Ralph said, 'If we're not careful he will be persuading us not to go ahead. He doesn't like there to be dissension in the village, wants us all to live in harmony. Well, I won't be dissuaded from going ahead. My mind's made up.'

'Ralph, I couldn't bear it if Peter didn't like what we were doing.'

'Between the two of you, nothing controversial will ever get done. It's in the village interest for us to do what we said, believe me.'

'But if no one speaks to us . . .'

'They will, don't worry.'

Come Sunday evening Jimmy, taking Sunday as a day off that week, was ensconced in his favourite spot in the bar, with a willing audience of Pat and Vera, eager to hear any gossip going the rounds. None of them had been in church that morning, but they had heard about Arthur's rebellion.

Pat didn't take long to air her views when the subject came up. 'How he dared do that I'll never know. What an embarrassment for Sir Ralph, eh?'

'A lot of venom there, yer see.' Jimmy rather knowingly tapped the side of his nose.

Pat bent forward so that she could hear better. 'When you tap your nose, I *know* you've got a tale to tell. Go on then.'

'Yes, venom, stands to reason.'

'What stands to reason, what are yer talking about? Have they had a row before, then?'

'I can see you 'aven't 'eard. Here's Willie, he knows more than me – come and sit with us Sylvia, while 'e gets the drinks in.' Sylvia came across and greeted them all as she sat down. Vera shuffled further along the settle to make room for her. 'We're talking about Arthur and the collection plate this morning.'

'I know! I didn't know where to look. I thought the rector dealt with it wonderfully. Willie was furious. Opening up old wounds, he called it. Do you know what he meant, Jimmy?'

'I do, and that's a fact.'

Pat, fast losing her temper with all the secrecy, said, 'Will someone tell me what's going on please?'

Jimmy wanted to wait until Willie joined them.

'Well–l–l–l–l?' Pat said.

'Go on, Willie, you tell her about Arthur.'

Willie appeared to be weighing the matter up, and then he decided to speak. 'I'm amazed yer don't know. Arthur is a relative of Ralph's.'

Pat and Vera were scandalised. Pat was the first to recover. 'A relative of Sir Ralph's? Never! How can he be? On his father's side he's a Prior from down Shepherd's Hill, on his mother's side he's a Goddard, and his wife's a daughter of the old headmaster of the Grammar School in Culworth. 'Ow can 'e be a relative?'

Willie took a deep draught of his pint and began his story. 'Ralph's grandfather was a right well set up young man, handsome yer know. Sir Bernard, he was called. Well, he was an army officer and he fought in the Boer War. They do say . . .'

'How do you know all this?' Pat queried.

''Cos my grandma was a young woman at the time and she knew all about it. They do say that he was a right ladies' man. No one was safe if he took a fancy to 'em, from servant girls to high society. A right charmer he was and not half. Well, his parents persuaded him to get married, calm 'im down a bit they thought, put a stop to the scandal and that. He married just as the Boer War started, goes off after a few days' honeymoon to serve Queen and country in South Africa. Gets wounded, gets sent home. Right glamorous he looks with his arm in a sling and a walking stick 'cos of his bad leg. Goes back after a few months' recuperation, leaves Lady Templeton expecting, and what no one realised until later, he leaves Mrs Beattie Prior expecting too.'

Vera sat back amazed. 'No!! It all went on then just like it does now, it's no different is it?'

'Beattie Prior's husband was right set up, thinking that after ten years of being married he'd at last proved himself. Well, 'e 'ad dark hair, really dark hair, and she was dark like a Spaniard.'

'What's that got to do with it?' Pat asked.

'You'll see. One night there's this terrible thunderstorm, the night that big branch fell from the royal oak and they all thought it would die. That same night Beattie and Lady Templeton both 'ad their babies. The doctor attended at the Big House, and the old woman who acted as village midwife attended Beattie. They both had boys at dawn within an hour of each other. It was only when Prior saw the Templeton baby at its christening that his suspicions were really aroused. They had a big do yer see, 'im being the son and heir, and all the village was invited. So there's Beattie Prior standing there with 'er little lad in her arms and her husband beside her and up comes Lady Templeton with her little lad in *her* arms. Both babies were as fair as it's possible to be, with dark brown eyes like all the Templetons. So alike they could 'ave been twins! Arthur's grandad looked first at one and then at the other and so did Lady Templeton and snap! The terrible truth dawned.'

Drink forgotten, Pat said, 'What happened then?'

'Don't know. It was all hushed up. All I can say is that Beattie Prior and her husband suddenly moved into their farm down the bottom of Shepherd's Hill. Up till then they'd been as poor as crows, 'im only a labourer on Home Farm. Sir Bernard and his wife 'ad another two boys after that first one. Anyway, First World War put a stop to it, 'cos Sir Bernard got killed and his son did too. Only just seventeen he was, lied about his age when he joined up.'

Pat shook her head. 'I don't believe a word of it, you've made it up. Arthur Prior a Templeton! That's a laugh.'

'I'm telling you the tale as my grandma told me, and she wasn't a liar.'

'So,' said Vera, 'Arthur is the son of that Beattie's baby?'

'That's right.'

'So,' said Pat, 'Arthur Prior is a kind of cousin to Sir Ralph?'

'I think that's what he'll be.'

'Does Sir Ralph know all this?'

'I don't know, no one mentions it any more.'

'Well, by heck, what a story. No wonder he's against Sir Ralph making more money. He's jealous, that's what. Maybe he thinks he ought to own the spare land. Maybe he thinks his eldest ought to inherit from Sir Ralph with him having no children. Maybe he even thinks he ought to be *Sir Arthur*.' She giggled at the thought. 'I wonder which one was born first? That could make a difference, could it?'

"Ere, wet yer whistle with another drink. My round.' The three women pushed their glasses towards Jimmy and while he got the drinks in they sat contemplating the implications of what they had just heard.

Sylvia asked Willie if he remembered both of them at school.

'Oh yes. Ralph as bright as it's possible to be, always leading, always ahead, always thinking up tricks to play and Arthur, good old Arthur sensibly plodding along. As kids we didn't know any of the history of course. It never dawned on us.'

'I tell you what Willie, maybe your Sylvia's married into the aristocracy!'

Sylvia laughed. 'Sir Willie! Surely not!'

'What d'yer mean?'

'I mean that maybe your dad was one of Sir Bernard's mistakes, yer never know, with 'im spreading it about so much!'

Willie took offence. 'That's enough, Pat, thank you, I'll have you know my grandmother was a Methodist, strict teetotal she was. Never a drop.'

'Can't say you've inherited her qualities! This building of the houses could be quite a story before the year's out, couldn't it? Wait till the papers get on to it!'

After the evening service Peter went home, changed from his cassock into a shirt and jeans, and went downstairs to spend time with Caroline. It being summer, they had left their evening meal until evensong was over and the children in bed. Caroline had pulled the dining table closer to the french windows to catch what small amount of breeze there was, and the two of them sat eating their supper together.

'Too hot for cooking tonight, hope you don't mind a salad.'

'Of course I don't mind. It's a prince of a salad and delicious. I've been thinking, my darling girl, it's time we had a Sunday morning crèche.'

'I had the very same thought myself, in fact someone mentioned it when I was shaking hands after the service. They said there's our two, there's baby Frances, and there's the four Nightingales, and that's just for starters. They can't possibly come with four of them, so, yes, something will have to be done. We'll need toys and things to keep them busy, a room and a rota for helpers.'

'I'll leave that to you, then. Although it's sweet of Alex to shout "Dada", it's not conducive to worship, is it? He must be distracting for other people besides me.'

'Yes, I'm sure he must be, but in the nicest way.'

'Yes, of course. Caroline, do you ever feel a little worried by Beth?'

'Worried? What about?'

'Well, she seems so quiet. She tags along behind Alex like a shadow. He's talking and making himself a nuisance, but Beth is so quiet. Those big blue eyes of hers take everything in but she doesn't talk and I mean! Going to sleep as soon as she sees me come in!'

'Are you saying you think she's retarded?'

'No, no, not at all, but there is something worrying me, and I'm not sure what.'

'You used the words "takes everything in" – you're right, she does. If I say I want something and it's within her reach, she goes straight to it and brings it to me. If I say it's bathtime she's half way up the stairs before you can say knife. If I've mislaid something she knows exactly where it is and takes me to it. She's not daft, believe me, just overshadowed by Alex.'

'I see. Well she is only nineteen months, so we'll give it a bit longer.'

'You watch, she'll surprise us all.'

Peter offered Caroline more potatoes. She shook her head. 'No, you finish them, I have enough. Peter, what do you think is behind that scene in church?'

'I'm convinced it isn't just the houses. You should have seen the look they gave each other, something goes very deep between the two of them. Arthur said he disliked Ralph's Lord of the Manor look, which I thought very scathing. No doubt, my darling girl will find out before she is much older.'

'No doubt she will.'

'I'm most concerned about these houses, though. Ralph is determined to go ahead with his plans, but I'm not too sure they could . . .'

'I think the whole matter depends on how many houses are built. Six or eight or even ten for renting would be ideal, but twenty or more would throw the whole village out of balance, and I would feel I should protest.'

'I don't know if we can get involved. I'd rather work from the sidelines to influence things. We certainly can't align ourselves with Arthur Prior's petition, nor with Ralph.'

'Why not?'

Peter, noting the challenging tone of Caroline's voice, searched for a diplomatic reply. 'Unfortunately, you and I have people from both persuasions under our care and we can't be seen to side with either, I have to do what's right by both of them.'

'I know.'

'You won't take sides will you?'

'I might.'

'Caroline!'

'I only said I might.'

'Look, we had all that trou . . . misunderstanding about Jimmy and his rabbit snares, please don't, darling, please don't begin another crusade.'

'Crusade? Well, really!'

'I mean it, Caroline, everything is going so well at the moment. The attendance figures are way up, all the things I've started are taking shape, and I don't want anything to mar it.'

Caroline left her chair and went to sit on his knee. 'Move round; that's it. It's ages since I sat on your knee. You and I promised we wouldn't trespass.'

'Yes, I know, but . . . ' He couldn't go further because Caroline was kissing him.

'Peter, let's leave all this and go to bed.'

'You abandoned woman you, what will Sylvia think in the morning when she comes?'

'"Good on yer, Pete," she'll say!'

'You've watched too many Australian soap operas.'

'When do I get time to watch soap operas?'

'Never.'

'You lock up, I'll go up to bed.' Caroline trailed her fingers along his bruised jaw. 'Handsome man you are, did you know that? Handsome.' She got off his knee, kissed his cheek and ran up the stairs.

Peter decided he'd clear the table and stack the dishwasher. After he'd turned out the lights, checked the cats were in and the doors were locked, he followed her upstairs. Caroline was standing looking at herself in the mirror. The clothes she'd been wearing lay in a heap at her feet.

'Peter, I'm getting old. Look, everything I possess is beginning to sag.'

He kicked her clothes aside and stood behind her, locking his hands around her waist. She smelt of soap and toothpaste. She must have had a shower, for her skin was warm but at the same time slightly damp. Speaking to her reflection in the mirror Peter said, 'You look wonderful to me, and quite superbly tempting, Dr Harris. What's made you decide to take stock?'

He watched his own hands as they began to wander about her body, enjoying the feel of her smooth flesh. He bent to kiss the nape of her neck where her hair curled childlike against her skin, and he looked over her shoulder into the mirror to observe her reaction. She rested her body against

143

his and taking his hand she held it to her breast, smoothing her fingers along the back of it, enjoying its strength, and twisting his wedding ring round and round. Then she took his hand to her mouth and gently kissed each of his fingers.

Peter turned her around and, with the same fingers she had kissed, began slowly tracing her profile from where her forehead began at her hairline, down her nose, her top lip, across her mouth and down her chin to her jaw. Then cradling her face in his hands, he caressed her mouth with long awakening kisses. He stopped, and looking deeply into her eyes said, 'You don't regret marrying me, do you, darling? I do realise it does put limitations sometimes on your reaction to things, doesn't it?'

'I don't regret one single minute of the time I've spent with you. It's not the easiest of occupations being a clergy wife, but the one particular member of that august body I've married makes all the limitations worthwhile. Mind you, I can't guarantee there will never come a time when I shan't put my foot down on some principle or another.' She grinned at him and said, 'I might even sign Arthur Prior's petition!'

He stopped kissing her and scrutinised her face. She laughed and so did he.

'Get thee to bed, woman of my heart.'

Chapter 15

Pat placed herself next to Vera on the settle and put her orange juice down on the nearest beer mat. Vera inspected her glass and said 'Orange juice! Since when 'ave you, Pat Duckett, drunk orange juice? That's a turn-up for the book.'

'Mi dad's 'ere, isn't he? Staunch teetotal he is, Lord 'elp us. Went on the bottle when mum died, straight down the slippery slope. Alcoholic he was and no mistake. Took himself in hand and hasn't touched a drop since. We shan't be seeing him in 'ere, believe me.'

Jimmy expressed himself as being disappointed. 'Fancied 'aving another chap to talk to, make a change from all you women.'

'Cheek. At least you get to know all the latest. That taxi job of yours takes up all yer time. There's only me and Vera to tell you anything. Isn't it hot tonight? Hardly slept a wink last night, tossing and turning, all the windows open and I was still too hot. Mind you, with our Michelle's bed in my room and her restless too, I didn't have much hope.'

'So, what is the latest then?'

'Well.' Pat took a long draught of her orange juice and

pulled a face. 'I shan't last long on this game. It's only a token gesture to mi dad. Well, little Flick is doing fine. Been home two weeks now. Did yer see 'er this morning, sitting out in the sun watching your geese? Well, yer wouldn't 'cos yer were working, but she was. Two crutches she has, bless her heart. Jimbo, I call him that now, we're very close . . . '

'Close? You and Mr Charter-Plackett? That's rich!' Vera shook her head at this flight of fancy on her friend's part.

'Less of yer cheek, Vera Wright. I'm one of his most reliable staff. He's told me so. And now mi dad's come I shall be doing more work for him. So . . . '

Jimmy interrupted. 'You were telling us about little Flick.'

'Right, I was. Jimbo was saying she's so disappointed not to have got back to school in time for the start of term, but she's determined she'll be back before long. Mr Palmer says she can go mornings at first and see how she gets on. She goes for therapy in the afternoons. She adores that baby. And no wonder, that little Fran is beautiful. I could take 'er 'ome with me.'

'Yer'd soon change yer mind.'

Pat laughed. 'Yes, I expect I should! She 'asn't 'alf got some grit she 'as, that Flick. When yer think 'ow badly knocked about she was, and 'ere she is fighting to get back to school. Jimbo, as I call 'im now, is that anxious about 'er. But then so would I be if it was our Michelle.'

'I've been thinking, where's yer dad sleeping?'

Pat's face fell. 'With our Dean. He's none too pleased and I don't suppose mi dad is either, 'aving to share with a teenager.'

'Where yer working this week?' Vera asked, wondering if she might offer her services. Cleaning at the nursing home didn't bring in that much.

'We've a twenty-first dinner party at a big house far side of Culworth on Saturday, a fiftieth wedding anniversary lunch Sunday, and then Friday night Little Dereham's Cricket Club annual dinner. That'll be a right smashing do and not half. They're a right crowd. Then we've a special dinner up at the Big House for Craddock Fitch coming up soon. He's entertaining some of the local nobs. But I'm not helpin' with that.'

'Trying to ingratiate himself, is 'e?' Jimmy asked.

'Something like that. Doing overkill to make up for wanting to sell the silver.'

'What does yer Dad do for a living then?' Jimmy asked.

'Up till now he's been in charge of the glasshouses at Bothring Park. Grapes, peaches, melons, you name it he grew 'em. I've asked Venetia if there's a job going up at the Big House, but I haven't heard anything positive.'

'Leastways he'll get your garden in order,' was Vera's heartfelt comment. 'My Don's sick of all them seeds from your weeds blowing into our garden, one body's work it is weeding.'

'If that's all yer've got to worry about I feel sorry for yer.'

Jimmy, seeing a row blowing up, offered to get the drinks in.

Pat spotted Willie coming in. 'Oh there's Willie, he's been in court today. Come on over Willie, and tell us 'ow yer went on,' she shouted.

After he'd settled himself in his usual chair he said, 'My Sylvia's babysitting tonight, the rector and Dr Harris have gone to a big dinner at the Deanery. So I shan't stay long, I'll go keep her company.'

'We know, we know, tell us 'ow yer went on at the court.'

'Well . . . them who stole the lead from the church roof got fined and community service. Ought to have been horsewhipped, stealing, but there you are. You might say I caught 'em too early, if they'd stolen more they'd have been fined more, might even have gone to prison.'

'No, really, is that all they got?'

'But . . . ' said Willie, 'there's more.' He glanced round the bar. 'Guess whose case was before mine?'

'No idea. Whose was it?'

'Alan Crimble's.'

Pat nearly jumped from her seat. 'We haven't seen 'im serving tonight yet, 'e didn't get prison did he?'

'No. Asked a policeman I know from Culworth. "What did the last one get?" I says to 'im. "Not enough," he says.' Willie took another drink. Vera and Pat became impatient.

'Well, what did he get?'

'He got fined three hundred pounds, disqualified from driving for a year. He can pay the three hundred pounds off at so much a week. Car's a write-off of course, it was that before the accident anyways, we all knew that.'

'So are you saying, then, that Flick getting hurt like she did, didn't count?'

'Well, yer see for a start, there were no witnesses, were there? Middle of the morning, everyone in school, or out at work, and pouring with rain, yer know, nobody about, and she did run out from the gate without looking, she said so herself to the police, she told 'em when she was well enough to speak to 'em. Rector and I ran out *after* we'd 'eard the crash, so we didn't see it either. So it's all the legal things he copped for. No MOT, no insurance, no road fund licence and that.'

'Well, at least the roads will be safe for us to go out on for a year, that's something I suppose.' Pat suddenly put her head down and muttered, 'Don't look now, he's just come in.'

Jimmy shouted, 'Any chance of a lift, Alan? Mi battery's flat!'

Georgie's head came up and the pint glass she was filling overflowed. She served her customer, took the money, and came over to see Jimmy.

'That's enough Jimmy, he's been tried, got his punishment and now the matter is closed.'

'You might call it closed, Georgie, but I bet Harriet and Jimbo and little Flick don't call it closed. She's still struggling on crutches, but I notice Alan's walking OK. Looks to me like he's got off scot free in comparison.'

'Don't you think that perhaps Alan is feeling bad about all this? He doesn't exactly enjoy knocking down a child, you know. One day, Jimmy, it might be you who knocks down a child, and then see how you feel about it!' Georgie turned on her heel and marched back behind the bar. She left Jimmy still of the opinion that he was right.

Alan began serving. Bryn and Georgie were glad of his help, for the beautiful weather had brought out the crowds. Some customers had driven from as far as Culworth to sit out in the little courtyard and enjoy the summer's evening, or on the green or at the little tables Bryn had put outside the door. They encroached on the road a little but the sergeant turned a blind eye on hot summer nights. Bryn and Georgie and Alan were all kept busy serving, and the dining room was busy too; altogether the three of them were very pleased with the atmosphere and especially the frequent pinging of the till.

A young man came to the bar for six lagers. Alan gave him a tray, he paid for them and wandered off outside, balancing the tray carefully as he squeezed between the crowded tables. Jimmy watched him leaving and said, 'Isn't that chap a friend of them that punched the rector?'

'Can't be,' said Pat, 'they were banned.'

'I don't think he was 'ere that night. But I've definitely seem 'im in Culworth with 'em, boating on the river and causing a lot of annoyance with being daft. I recognise 'is funny haircut.'

Alan set off around the tables collecting the used glasses. He went to the bar with several and then Bryn said to him, 'There must be a lot outside, Alan, go take a look, we're running really short in here.'

It was the loud shouting which drew the attention of everyone inside the bar. Bryn looked at Georgie and then hastily pushed his way outside. The noise was becoming louder and louder and then they heard the crashing of chairs, and women screaming. Jimmy, Vera and Pat, being seated close to one of the exits, were the first of the concerted rush of customers to get outside to see what was happening. A whole group of lads had Alan on the ground and were kicking him. He was trying to protect his face and head with his hands, but they were kicking from all sides and he'd no chance of escape. Bryn muscled in, and with the help of some law-abiding customers they managed to pull Alan away, but then punches began flying and Bryn was unable to control the ensuing fight. Inside, Georgie had rung for the police, and those customers nervous of getting involved had spread out onto the green to avoid getting hurt.

Pat helped Alan inside. The cut he'd received in the accident was nothing to the condition his face was in after the kicking. Despite her anger at what Alan had done to Flick, she couldn't help feel sorry for him.

'Here, Georgie, you got a cloth or something? There's blood all over the place. Quick, be quick, it's running all down 'is shirt.' Georgie came with a tea cloth and between them they mopped his face. But he winced and protested so much at the pain they caused, they had to desist and leave him, slumped on a chair, holding the cloth to his face.

'Brandy, that's what he needs. Oh God, they're coming in 'ere now. Watch out.'

'Where is he, where is he?' Tables and chairs began crashing over, glasses and drink spilling all over the floor. The noise was almost more frightening than the fighting, and Pat wished the police would come pronto, but how many would it take to control this lot? The sergeant wouldn't be much good on his own.

Thankfully, the sound of a police siren pierced the air. Almost immediately the fighting stopped and there was a mass exodus of men. They struggled to reach the doors and get out before they got caught, but the doors were quickly secured and they were all confined in the bar. Two of the men headed for the gents', hoping to escape out of the lavatory window, but Georgie was standing in the passage waiting for them, brandishing a cricket bat.

'Oh, no, you don't! One step and I'll clobber you with this and I mean it.' She raised the cricket bat, ready to strike. They went forward with the intention of taking the bat from her, but the glint in her eye stopped them. 'You've done enough damage, and you're getting the book thrown at you. Get back in that bar.' She stepped forward holding the bat with both hands at shoulder level. Withering under her determined gaze, the two of them backed off. Georgie followed them, holding the bat at the ready.

Above the din she shouted, 'Officer! These two are the ringleaders, I've just stopped them trying to escape.' Everyone stopped what they were doing and looked at her. Petite and pretty with her fine delicate blonde hair, her eyes blazing in defence of Alan, the cricket bat held aloft, she made an arresting picture. Bryn came to take the bat from her, and as he did so her anger melted and she clutched Bryn's arm.

'Oh help, Bryn, I'm going to make a fool of myself. I'm going to be sick.' She disappeared behind the bar.

Before the police left, the senior officer had a word with Bryn.

'You'll have to look to your laurels, Mr Fields, this is twice in quick succession we've had to come to a brawl here, and this one is much more serious that the last. Better control, if you please. Or else next time your licence comes up for renewal it might be . . .' He drew his finger across his throat, making his meaning very clear.

Bryn grimly apologised. Losing his temper with the police would gain nothing. He was so angry with himself for not realising that the banned drinkers were actually on his premises. One of the men involved in the fighting volunteered to take Alan to casualty. Georgie saw him into the car, supplying him with a clean towel to hold to his face. 'Now take care Alan, get the hospital to ring us if there's any problems, won't you? Best of luck, love.' Alan nodded; he couldn't speak because his face was rapidly swelling.

The customers began trailing back inside to finish their drinks, but the overturned tables and chairs, the broken glass and spilled drinks made it impossible.

'This would never 'ave 'appened when Betty MacDonald was 'ere. She'd 'ave cracked their heads together, clasped 'em to 'er bosom and thrown 'em out,' Vera observed.

Pat laughed. 'Well, you should know Vera, she threw you out once.'

Vera laughed, wagged her finger at Pat and went home.

★

Alan came back from the hospital the following day. His nose was broken, he had several teeth missing at the front, two cuts which had needed stitches, and his whole face was badly swollen and bruised. In trying to protect his head, his hands had taken a lot of the punishment and they were bruised and swollen too, with three fingers broken. His back and chest were painful from bruising, making it difficult for him to move. After Georgie had got him to bed, she and Bryn held a council of war in their little office.

'I don't care what you say, Georgie, we can't have him serving in the bar for a long time, if ever again.'

Georgie pushed her hair back from her face and pleaded. 'What's he going to do if he doesn't work for us? You know full well he's not capable of standing on his own two feet, he needs us. We've looked after him for sixteen years, it'll be cruel to have to tell him he's to go. I could have killed those two last night.'

'I could see that. You looked full of fight.'

'I felt scared.'

'No matter how we feel about Alan, our customers don't want him here. In a big city he wasn't nearly so noticeable, but here his idiosyncrasies seem magnified. There is no way that we can sacrifice our livelihood to Alan. I know he's useless without us, but he's got to go, so you must make your mind up to it. The insurance will go mad when we send this claim in. Our premium will rocket, and we'll be working to pay the premiums instead of working to make a profit. We're in business, Georgie, we're not running a home for the inadequate.'

'Inadequate! That's unkind!'

'We were up till two this morning clearing up the mess, so I'm not in the mood for being magnanimous, believe me.'

Georgie put her arm through Bryn's. 'Can't I persuade you, not even one little teeny bit?' She smiled up at him, brushed a finger along his moustache and tweaked his cheek, but he didn't smile back.

'No, sorry, and at bottom you know the decision is right. I'll get in touch with that girl from Penny Fawcett who asked us for a job, and we'll give her an interview.'

'We can't turn him out till he's better and he's found somewhere else.'

'Of course not. I'm not that ruthless.'

Chapter 16

Because of the Indian summer, Muriel was getting out of bed much earlier than usual to walk Pericles before the real heat of the day began. He was finding the hot weather almost unbearable and some days she felt real concern on his behalf. They walked slowly, in deference to his age, along Jacks Lane and down towards Shepherd's Hill. Pericles' nose began twitching and so did Muriel's. She was certain she could smell cooking, surely they weren't already working in the kitchens at the back of the Store? Seven o'clock? Surely not.

Pericles pulled on the lead, wanting a chance to investigate the smells.

'Pericles, all you think of nowadays is your stomach. You're getting very greedy.' As she crossed Shepherd's Hill, Muriel realised that something odd was afoot. She rounded the corner of the Methodist chapel, now boarded up prior to demolition, and gasped at what she saw. 'Oh, dear. No! Oh dear. Come! Heel, Pericles.'

Dotted here and there, on the grass between the trees, were parked ramshackle caravans, old converted buses and an assortment of motorised vehicles. There were dogs and children playing, in front of some fires were burning, and the whole paraphernalia of permanent outdoor existence lay around. As she stood mesmerised by all the activity, two men came towards her each carrying large pickaxes. As they reached her they said: 'Morning missus, nice day.'

'Yes, it is.' They passed her and went directly to the chapel, and began attacking the boarding nailed over the back door.

'That's private property, it was a chapel.'

'Not no more it ain't,' one of the men shouted, and continued his attack on the boarding. Two of the big dogs came rushing at Pericles. Muriel picked him up and the dogs began leaping at her to reach him. Pericles struggled with fright, and Muriel shouted. One of the men with a pickaxe bawled at the dogs, 'Give over.' But they didn't stop and he came across and hit them with the handle of his axe. They scurried away howling. 'Don't worry missus, they mean no harm. Let him off, he'll be all right.'

But Muriel hurried away. She crossed the green to give Pericles a chance to run about a little and then hurried back to Ralph.

'Ralph, Ralph are you up?' He was just coming downstairs. 'Oh, Ralph, there you are.'

'My dear, how did you get your dress so dirty? And . . . '

'Never mind about my dress, there are travellers camped on the spare land. Dozens of them with big dogs and they're breaking into the chapel. Oh Ralph, I was so frightened.'

Ralph put his arms around her and held her tightly. 'This *is* a pretty kettle of fish and no mistake. They didn't hurt you, did they?'

'Oh no, it was the dogs jumping up that dirtied my

dress. What are we going to do Ralph?'

'When you say travellers, how many are you talking about?'

'There must be at least a dozen vehicles, possibly more, and there's loads of people and children and dogs, and there's all their things lying about. Everywhere is littered. Where on earth have they come from?'

'I don't know. I think I'll ring the police.'

'But the sergeant won't be able to do anything all by himself, there's so many of them.'

'We'll see. I'll ring him now. They must have moved in during the night, they weren't there at ten last night when we walked Pericles, were they?'

'Not a sign. I'll make your breakfast while you ring him.'

When the telephone rang, the sergeant was half way through his porridge, and he did enjoy it. He loved the rich dark swirls of black treacle contrasting with the bland flavour of the porridge as it passed over his taste buds. Now, with the phone ringing, it would be turning into a dark brown grey mush and he felt aggrieved.

As he listened to Sir Ralph telling him the bad news, he undid the top button of his pyjamas to give himself more air. He didn't relish this idea at all. Oh no. He'd need reinforcements, yes, definitely reinforcements.

'Certainly, Sir Ralph, I'll get onto it straight away.' Well, when I've finished my porridge that is, he thought. He sat down again, spooned the porridge into his mouth as fast as he could, drank his mug of tea down as quickly as possible, why did she always make it so hot? and raced into the bedroom to get dressed.

His wife called out. 'You'm can't go out on duty not shaved. Sir Ralph won't like that at all 'e won't, now will 'e?

Only cause trouble you not being shaved, his lordship'll report you, he will, definite.'

He raced angrily into the bathroom and straight off cut his chin with his razor. This wasn't his day.

Sir Ralph was waiting for him. He got out his notebook. As soon as he saw the vehicles and the dogs he said, 'I recognise this lot. They've been camped on Arthur Prior's land for the last three weeks. In his back field down the old cart track. Wonder what made 'em move 'ere.'

Wryly Ralph said, 'I wonder.'

The sergeant looked at him. 'You thinking what I'm thinking, Sir Ralph?'

'Could be,' he answered. 'Well, what shall we do then?'

'First, they're in trouble for breaking and entering the chapel, and damaging trees what have a preservation order on 'em, look, they've chopped off them branches for their fire. I think we shall have to get Culworth to come, it's too big a job for one man this is. Two of these chaps have been up for grievous but they got off scot free, not enough evidence, but we knew they'd done it all right. Leave it to me, sir, best not get involved. You're the landowner now, I reckon.'

'I am, yes.'

'Right. I'll let you know.'

Close to the chapel a small crowd was watching events.

'Who is they, Sir Ralph?'

'Just travellers. They've broken into the chapel . . . '

'Oh no, the devils, what will they do next?'

'I sawed them in Arthur Prior's fields last week, made a right mess there, they have.'

'We shan't sleep safe in our beds. Better lock all the doors.'

'Yer right there. And windows. And keep yer cats in,

case they run short of food.'

'Oh, don't be disgusting.'

'You mark my words.'

Malcolm the milkman stopped his van, and lifted a crate off the back.

'You're not selling 'em milk are yer Malcolm?'

'I've a living to earn, if they want milk and they pay me for it, milk they'll get. 'Scuse me, let me through.'

'Yer encouraging 'em, you are. Yer a traitor.'

'We want rid of 'em.'

'He can wait for his money this week, rotten little money grabber he is.'

Ralph stalked home. 'MURIEL! Where are you?'

'Here, dear. What's happening?'

'I'm going down to see Arthur Prior, he's at the bottom of this.'

'Why? Why has he done it?'

'You don't know? Of course you don't. I'll tell you the whole story about my dear cousin Arthur.' Ralph didn't make any bones about telling her. Her hand to her mouth she listened, horrified.

'So there you have it. Mainly revenge for past wrongs, I think,' Ralph concluded.

'Oh, Ralph, my dear, it's not your fault. You weren't even born and neither was he, and they did get a farm of their own, something they would never have been able to aspire to. Well, I never knew all this before. How long have you known?'

'My father told me when I started at the village school when I was four, he thought I should be forewarned in case anything was said. He found the right words to explain it and somehow I didn't find it dirty or nasty, because he told me so beautifully. No one at school ever mentioned it to me and I never did to Arthur, it didn't seem right somehow.'

'I should think not indeed.'

'So there you have it. I shall not give up. He can be as obstructive as he likes, I will still go ahead, because I know it is a good thing for the village and that's my concern, not Arthur Prior's hurt feelings or his jealousy.'

'That's what it is, isn't it, jealousy? He feels his father was as much a Templeton as any born with the name. He feels bitter inside.'

'It must have been a shock to him when I came back, after all those years away.'

'Of course, yes, they were invited to our evening wedding party and never came, said they already had an engagement elsewhere, so that explains it. I expect he's angry that you've been found to own land, when he thought all that side of the family wealth was over and done with. He's got two sons, hasn't he?'

'He has. Both sons work the farm with him. There is another aspect to this though.'

'What?'

'The farm belongs to them only so long as there is a Prior working the land and living on the farm. As soon as that stops, the farm comes to me or any person named Templeton alive at the time.'

'You mean they don't *own* it?'

'No, they pay a small rent each year to the family solicitor, something like twenty-five pounds. A kind of token. It's been twenty-five pounds all these years.'

'I see. That must be galling for Arthur. Very galling. Working hard and yet never his own. I expect he must have in his blood what you have in yours, a deep-seated satisfaction from owning land.'

'Yes, I think perhaps you could be right there.'

'Ralph, it seems odd they were given a farm so close to the village.'

'Well, at the time, being almost in Little Derehams was a long way away.'

'Yes, of course, it would be almost an hour's walk away, far enough I suppose. No one knew then that Turnham Malpas would become the centre of things, having the only church and the only school and the only Store, because they had their own then, didn't they? Actually, I'm beginning to feel quite sorry for Arthur.'

Ralph stood up and leant over her to kiss her cheek. 'You have a kind heart, my dear. A very kind heart, and I love you for it. Now I'm going to see Arthur to give him a piece of my mind. I'll teach him to meddle in my affairs. Who the devil does he think he is?'

Muriel ran after him down the garden path. 'Please, Ralph, don't be hasty, dear, come back in and we'll talk about it some more.'

'No, my dear, I'm going. Shan't be long.' She watched him back the Mercedes out of the garage and roar off down Pipe and Nook Lane, far faster than was safe. She ran through the house again and out of the front door signalling him to stop, but he raced past the front of the house ignoring her shouts.

He'd never been to the Prior's farm in all his life. Delicacy forbade it. But there it was, 'Prior's Farm' painted on a smart swinging board at the entrance, He turned right and slowly made his way up the well-tended farm lane into the yard.

Even the best run farms usually have old equipment lying about, or hay scattered around the yard, but not here. Everywhere was immaculate. Except for the distant mooing of cows, it was almost impossible to imagine that a real live working farm was being run there. Every piece of woodwork was smartly painted, every door hung straight, beside each door were half barrels painted and filled with flowers. A sheepdog came good-naturedly up to him, wagging its tail. He bent to pat its head.

A curtain moved slightly; someone was watching them. He rang the door bell. No one answered, but Ralph heard footsteps approaching from behind.

'Yes, and what do you want? Come to view another of your properties, have you?'

Arthur Prior in corduroy trousers, matching cap and a plaid workman's shirt, stood legs apart, arms folded, awaiting a reply. The two men faced each other. Both stockily built, both white haired, both with the long aristocratic nose of the Templetons and each utterly determined to have his own way.

'No, I've come to see you.'

'Well I'm here, fire away.'

'I understand you have some travellers on your land.'

'Did have.'

'Right, did have. Was it you persuaded them to camp on the spare land during the night?'

'Now, as if I'd do a thing like that to you.'

'That's not an answer.'

'Maybe not, but it's all you're going to get.'

'Some kind of joke, is it?'

'What?'

'Persuading them to move?'

'Don't know nothing about it. Got up this morning and lo and behold they'd gone. Couldn't believe my eyes, I couldn't.'

'I bet.'

'Betting man are you, then?'

'Not specially.'

'I'll bet you a thousand pounds you won't get houses built on that land.'

'I wouldn't allow you to lay such a bet when I know I shall win.'

'You bloody well won't win.' Arthur stepped closer. He prodded Ralph's lapel with his strong brown finger. 'Not this time, Ralphie boy, not this time. You and your family have had it your own way round here for generations, but now it's my turn.'

'Houses to rent for country people is wrong, is it?'

'You making money hand over fist is what's wrong. You've enough money, what do you want more for? You'll get planning permission, then sell the land, pocket the money and with a smile on your face like a Cheshire cat you'll be off to some far distant shore with that new wife of yours to spend the proceeds, leaving us with the rabble to contend with.'

'What I do is my affair. I don't have to justify myself to you.'

'Don't you indeed! Arrogant, that's what you are, arrogant. Want me to touch my forelock to you, like in the old days. Not me nor one of my sons will *ever* kowtow to you, Ralph Templeton, ever. So off my land . . .'

'That's the rub, isn't it? It's not your land, that's why you're taking this stand. The arrangement wasn't of my making, you know, nor of yours.'

'My father offered your father the money for this farm and he refused, refused to sell. Said it wasn't his to sell, he only held it for his descendants, so we're in a bind, aren't we?'

'I'm sorry, but, yes, you are. At the same time, you're making a good living from it. However, I really came about the travellers. Obviously it *was* you got them to move. But don't think this will stop me, nothing will. I'm determined to have my own way about those houses, and I will. Nothing will stop me. Nothing.'

'And I shall dance on your grave, you'll see, making money out of that land will be the end of you and yours, mark my words.' Arthur shook his fist at Ralph. Ralph made a dismissive gesture and left fuming.

Muriel had spent the time he was away dodging from one pathetic occupation to another. Nothing she did was right, and worst of all she'd broken one of her mother's china ornaments whilst she was dusting. It was of a small boy sitting on a tuffet with a bowl of soapy bubbles on his knee and a clay pipe almost falling out of his hand because he'd fallen asleep. She'd often wondered if her mother would have preferred a boy like this one, with his dark curls and his stubborn chin, instead of her. The sound of Ralph's car pulling up outside made her jump.

She hurried to open the door.

'Oh! Ralph! Are you all right? I've been so worried.'

'It's him, I knew it, as soon as I saw those – those travellers, I guessed. He won't beat me you know, he won't beat me, I'm determined to build those houses. The more he protests the more determined I shall become.' He went to the whisky decanter and poured himself a double.

'Oh Ralph dear, you don't normally drink at this time in the morning, is it wise?'

'I don't know what is wise any more.' Ralph went to sit at his desk, he put the glass down and said, 'Ralphie, he called me, Ralphie! I could throttle him.'

'Ralph, that's not very kind.'

'I don't feel kind this morning. He's deliberately persuaded those – those – people to move on to my land.

Purposely to cause me annoyance.'

'I'm sure it's quite by chance . . .'

'No, it's not, they were on his back field until last night, and this morning they have mysteriously moved onto mine.'

Not having witnessed Ralph in such a temper before, Muriel didn't know what to say next to calm him down. She flitted about the study wringing her hands. 'Ralph, dear, don't get too upset, I'm sure the police will sort it out eventually.'

'Oh eventually yes, months and months they'll take. It's the aggravation of it all I don't like. All we need is for the council to decide not to allow the application, and we shall be a laughing stock.'

'How can they refuse?'

'Because I agreed with you, and don't misunderstand me, you were absolutely right. I didn't let Neville Neal do his bit with the handouts to the appropriate councillors, so they'll get their revenge by refusing out of spite.'

'Well, what is to be, is to be. We shall just have to accept it.'

'The planning meeting is tonight, so we'll soon know. Neville said he'd give that councillor he is supposed to have in his pocket a ring after the meeting and find out what went on.'

'I didn't think you'd let Neville have anything more to do with it after I was so cross that day.'

'Oh, he's clinging on, he's wanting to invest in the project you see, tactfully suggested I might be over-stretched and he could help. The cheek of the man!'

'Will you be overstretched?'

'We, my dear, we. You and I know that we only intend building at the most eight houses, but we've applied for twenty, on the basis that if we ask for more than we want, we might eventually be allowed the eight we intended, and honour will be satisfied on both sides. So if that is the case, yes, we can afford it.'

'Ralph! How ingenious!' She stood in front of his desk, her hands leaning on the top, and said quietly, 'Do you think it might be possible to persuade the travellers to go without having to get the police in and everything get nasty? I saw some of the children, they do look in need of help, they really do. I would hate the thought of any of them getting hurt.'

'What would you have in mind, my dear?'

'Well, if Arthur Prior managed to get them to move, they must have moved for a very good reason. Do you suppose he gave them money? I can't think of any other way they might move willingly, can you?'

'Muriel! Now it's your turn to be a genius. Of course, that's the way. They'd have to move off first, then I'd give them the money and then we'd get someone to tip piles of earth at the entrance to stop the vehicles re-entering. Yes, how clever of you, my dear.'

'There's more than one way of skinning a cat, as my mother used to say.'

'How right she was. How very right. We'd have to go about it very subtly. If we weren't careful they'd agree to a sum and then haggle to get more and then more, and keep putting off the move. Yes, you've hit the nail on the head.' Ralph spent the morning laying his plans.

When the local paper came out on Thursday, large headlines declared that the planning committee had refused permission for the twenty houses. There were many reasons given, among them that they feared houses would mean a severe encroachment on the green belt, and of course such a large number of houses would involve cutting down far too many trees, added to which the whole balance of the village would be upset and it might mean the overloading of the village school, et cetera, et cetera. There was a quote from Arthur Prior, saying how pleased he was that the houses would not be built, and that it was a victory for common sense. When the reporter had interviewed Ralph he had tried to aggravate him into being angry and saying more than he intended, but Ralph had simply said how disapppointed he was, and that he would be trying again for permission at the earliest possible moment. There was also a small paragraph mentioning that the travellers were intending wintering in their new quarters. He decided not to attend church that Sunday and he and Muriel went out for the day instead. So he wasn't there to hear his telephone ring several times that day, and it was important too.

Chapter 17

Harriet had been awake with the baby since four am, so she was in no mood for the children playing up at breakfast time.

'If you two boys don't sit to the table by the time I've counted five I shall take steps.'

Flick was already seated, eating her cereal. 'I'm going to school this morning, coming home for my lunch.'

'Lovely darling, it's entirely up to you, you know that, but don't overdo things, will you? I'm counting! One, two, three, four . . . That's better. Now be quiet and eat. I've had a horrendous night with Fran and I'm in no mood for silly boys. Here you are. Jimbo! Never mind the post, please darling, sit down and eat.'

'Coming. God! I'm exhausted this morning. I'm sure Peter's added another mile to our run and not told me.'

'You exhausted? What were all the snores about then, around five o'clock?'

'Snores? I don't . . . I say look at this, an invite to dinner from old Fitch. Formal dress, two weeks on Friday. You know he asked me to cater for his special dinner party? Didn't realise we'd be included. Can't go. See to it, will you?'

'Can't go? Why not? Is that the night of the Freemasons' do? No, it's not, that's the following Friday. Finlay! Please! Butter your toast on your plate not on the tablecloth. Thank you. So we can go.'

'You know my rules.'

Harriet studied his reply for a moment. She knew his rules, but she'd been incarcerated with the family for four months now. With the baby, and with Flick needing so much care, she'd been absolutely nowhere at all. She needed, yes, desperately needed, to socialise.

'If I got mother to . . . '

'She won't and I don't want to leave Fran.'

'Jimbo, at this particular moment in time I could leave Fran on the nearest available doorstep. I've had it where she's concerned.'

Flick shrieked. 'Don't say that, please. She doesn't mean it, does she Daddy?'

Fergus, impatient of his little sister creating such a crisis, said, 'For heavens sake you know she doesn't. Don't be daft.'

Tears sprang to Flick's eyes. Jimbo patted her head and said, 'You know full well Mummy doesn't mean it. She's had a very bad night with Fran and she's worn out. You boys can get moving and clear your own dishes away for once. We've all got to pull together when Mummy's tired. I've got to get to the Store.'

He pushed his chair under the table and went to kiss Harriet. 'Love you, darling. Politically it wouldn't be good to refuse this invite, would it?'

'No.'

'Trouble is, if I go it would be like being on the rack, watching and not being able to jump in if things went wrong.' Neither of them had realised that Sadie had let herself in the house and was standing in the doorway waiting for a gap in the conversation.

'It's me. What's this invitation?'

Harriet explained.

'No problem there. I haven't received one, but then how can I? He doesn't know I exist. So you go and I shall hold the fort behind the scenes and make sure everything goes according to plan. What could be simpler?'

Harriet immediately felt better, till she remembered they'd then have no one to sit in.

'Ask Sylvia Biggs. She's used to looking after the rectory twins, she'd be all right with Frances.'

'Of course. Wonderful mother, you are. So resourceful.'

'Yes, I am. I'm a wonderful mother-in-law too, am I not Jimbo?' He went to kiss her, then said, 'Look, all this kissing is not getting the Store open. I'm going.'

'So am I. Shan't be in this morning, Jimbo dear, got an appointment in Culworth with my hairdresser. My roots are showing. I insist upon a kiss from all my grandchildren. Come, children, kiss your grandmother, starting with the eldest.'

After they had dutifully kissed her the boys escaped without taking away their dishes, and Flick began painfully trying to do it for them.

Harriet protested. 'No Flick, leave that. You've quite enough to do just getting ready for school. I'll see to it all.' Flick limped away. Once she was out of hearing Sadie said, 'I do hope that limp isn't going to be permanent.'

'Mother! It's only four months since the accident, they're mightily impressed at the hospital. They think she's doing brilliantly and so do we. Thanks for saving the day about the dinner, I'm dying to go.'

'You would have all these children Harriet, one would

have been quite sufficient considering the busy life you lead with the business. I told you so when Fergus was born, but oh no! Jimbo wanted a houseful because he'd known what it was like being an only one. But I can't see that you've suffered very much from being an only child.'

Frances' apologetic wail percolated into the kitchen. Sadie hastily picked up her bag. 'I'm going or I shall be late, I've got the first appointment. Bye!'

During the morning Jimbo learned they were not the only ones to get an invitation. Peter came in with some messages for him and mentioned that he and Caroline had been invited.

'Ah! Right. We have too. Harriet was thinking of asking Sylvia to sit in for us, Sadie can't because she's going to supervise for me while we play at being guests.'

'Not to worry. Willie is very good, he'll probably do it for us. The twins love him. We'll get something sorted. Is there a particular reason for this dinner, do you think?'

'I suspect he's wanting to make amends for the silver fiasco.'

'Yes, I expect so. I wonder if Ralph and Muriel have been invited? I don't suppose he'd want to go.'

'Look bad if he doesn't. Sheila Bissett and Ron have been invited. She's thrilled to bits. Been in this morning positively preening.'

'Actually she's not a bad sort you know.'

'That's magnanimous of you, considering the trouble she caused you.'

'We should have been honest in the first place. Must go, got lots to do. Bye Jimbo.' As Peter went to open the door to leave, Muriel came in. 'Good morning. God bless you, Muriel.'

She looked preoccupied. 'Oh, good morning Peter. Oh, dear. Oh, thank you.'

Jimbo came from behind the counter and pulled out a chair he kept for his customers' convenience.

'You look in need of a seat.'

Muriel looked puzzled. She glanced at the chair and promptly sat down rather heavily on it. 'Married life isn't all roses, is it Jimbo?'

'Oh dear!'

'Yes, oh dear. There's a lot of give and take, isn't there?'

'Oh yes. There is.'

'It's an invitation that came this morning. I say we should accept and Ralph, dear Ralph, says definitely no.'

'Is it for dinner at the Big House?'

'Oh! You've got one too?'

'Yes, and Peter, and Sheila Bissett.'

'Oh my word! Ralph says, you see, that under no circumstances can he face going up there again. He saw ghosts that day you all went to challenge Mr Fitch. He was very upset.'

'That's understandable.'

'But I do want to go. I can remember it you see, going in there when I was a little girl. His parents were lovely people. Out of the top drawer but so kindly. They never made you feel less than them. They never patronised.' She looked wistfully up at him. 'I would dearly love to go.'

'Getting quite a social butterfly, then?'

Muriel laughed. 'Remember your fortieth birthday dinner? I thought I would die of shyness that night. I expect if he did agree I'd be so scared on the night I wouldn't know what I was doing. I take up these challenges and then bitterly regret it.'

'Take some advice from a man with fourteen years

experience of married life. Don't mention it when you go back home. Give the matter a complete rest. Behave as if it never happened. Be all sweetness and light. Tonight prepare him his favourite dinner, and then . . . ' Jimbo cleared his throat. 'Well, the rest is up to you, but that's the moment to tell him how very much you want to go to the dinner. Catch him off his guard, if you see what I mean, when he's . . . well, when he's feeling mellow, as you might say.'

Muriel caught his eye and blushed. 'Jimbo!' She studied his idea for a moment and then said, 'I believe you could very well be right. I shall take your advice.'

'All part of the service. No charge! Did you come in to buy something?'

'Yes, but I can't remember what it was. I'll wander about a little and see if it comes back to me.'

From a sluggish start to the day business hotted up, and by lunchtime Jimbo was more than ready to leave the Store to his part-time assistant and go in the back for a quick bite to eat. He was sitting on his stool in the store room munching a pork pie which would be out of date by closing time, when he heard an excited voice shouting, 'Jimbo! Are you there?' It was Pat.

'In here, Pat, having lunch.'

'Can I come in?'

'Yes, come through.'

'Sorry about this, but I thought you'd like to hear my bit of good news. Mi dad's got the job up at the Big House.'

'Gardener, you mean?'

She nodded vigorously. 'First off he's to get the kitchen garden and the glasshouses in order, and then Jeremy says he'll see after that! You've no idea how pleased I am. Pay's good too. Dad wants our Dean to leave school and go work with him, but I'm not 'aving that and neither's Dean, he wants to stay on at school. Talk about relieved!'

'Relieved? I'm amazed!'

'Amazed? What for? What's happened?'

'Well, you've had a change of heart and no mistake.'

'Change of heart?'

'Yes. I thought Mr Fitch was public enemy number one as far as you were concerned.'

'Oh well, yes. I hadn't thought of it like that.'

'You certainly thought like that the night you and your Dean helped them with that effigy.'

'Effigy? Oh! you mean that dummy.' She scowled accusingly at him. ''Ow did you get to know it was me?'

Jimbo tapped the side of his nose with his forefinger and grinned. 'I have ways. Anyhow, you'll have to change your mind about him now, won't you? Now he's the saviour of the Duckett family.'

'I don't know about that. It's Jeremy's given him the job.'

'Believe me, Jeremy doesn't make a move without first consulting Mr Fitch, he has him on a very short lead. That's how the man works. I think you're all part and parcel of his new strategy to make amends for the silver débâcle.'

'Well, I don't care whether I am or not. If it gets Dad a job, that's what counts. Money talks.'

'Talking of money.' Jimbo reached into his desk and took out a clipboard crammed with papers. He flipped a few sheets over and then said, 'You OK for the Freemasons' dinner, and for a rugby annual dinner in Culworth, both on Fridays?'

'Yes, be glad to. Write the dates down for me and I'll put 'em in mi diary. You don't need me for the dinner up at the Big House then?'

'No, he's asked for waiters.'

'Pity! I'd have liked to be a fly on the wall! Who's going to be there?' Jimbo told her.

'Could be interesting, couldn't it? Sparks might fly, Sir Ralph going.'

'My mother-in-law will be in charge.'

'Whoever's working that night 'ad better watch it then. She's a tartar, she is. She misses nothing, she doesn't.'

'That's how it should be. We don't get asked again if things aren't absolutely perfect. It's people like you who help set the standard. You're good at your job, you know, Pat. Next time I have a small do I might give you a chance to show your mettle. Put you as senior waitress, see how you make out. With suitable remuneration, of course.'

'Really?'

'Oh yes. Reliable people, who know what they're doing and are willing to take responsibility, are few and far between, believe me.'

'Thank you Jimbo. Thank you very much.' Pat made to go and then came back in. 'You're right, I shouldn't let mi dad accept this job, should I?'

'Bleak economics dictate you should.'

'Yes, I really can't 'elp it, he's got to take it. Maddening though, isn't it, when money's your master.'

Chapter 18

The night before the travellers were expected to move off his land, Ralph found he couldn't sleep. Muriel's rest-lessness was one reason, and the other was apprehension as to whether or not they would really move. The money was safely tucked under his pillow.

'Ralph, I'm going to make a cup of tea, I simply can't sleep. Would you like one, dear?'

'Yes, please, and then I'm getting up. The tension is killing me.'

'And me.' They sat side by side in bed drinking their tea. Muriel looked at her little china alarm clock. Five thirty. Another hour and they'd be off. When she'd finished her tea she placed her cup on her bedside table and slid down under the bedclothes for five more minutes before getting up.

It was the loud hammering on their door which awakened them both.

Muriel checked the time. It was seven o'clock. 'Ralph! it must be them. We fell asleep.'

Ralph leapt out of bed, flung on his trousers and a sweater and raced downstairs, the money carefully hidden out of sight in his trouser pocket.

'Right guv, we're on the road. Not too early for you, are we?'

'No, not at all. You've all moved off?'

'Yes. Like we said.'

'Right, I'll walk round and take a look, if you don't mind.'

'Don't trust us, eh?'

'Something like that.'

'Got the money?'

'I have. It's yours when I'm sure everyone has gone.'

He walked steadily round the green and on to the land. From the side of the Methodist chapel he could see right across to the beck. Not a vehicle in sight, but what a mess. Tins and dead fires, newspapers, old rusting scrap metal, bin bags swollen with rubbish, branches of trees, sawn down but not used. Litter over the whole area. Ralph didn't care, they'd moved off.

The man who'd hammered so loudly on the door waited.

'Well, guv, I'm right you see, they've all gone like we promised. Money, money, money.' He rubbed his thumb and forefinger, together anticipating the feel of the paper in his hand.

Ralph took it from his pocket and began to count it out.

'No need for that, I know you'll be true to your word. Thanks.' He folded the roll of bank notes and stuffed it into his back pocket. Ralph watched him climb into his old lorry beside a woman, two children and a big dog. He flung it into gear and rumbled away down Shepherd's Hill.

So, this was his land. The mess they'd left behind couldn't spoil his pleasure. He saw the trees, ancient, gnarled, undisturbed for centuries, unconcerned that they had lost some branches, for their powerful life force would overcome their loss of limbs. The beck babbled along the stones, not so deep as usual with the long hot summer they'd had. The willows providing welcome shade for the fishes still swimming along as they had done when he was a little boy. His father had brought him down here and they'd fished with a little net for minnows. What joy that had given him. Now it was all his, all his. Arthur Prior wasn't going to win. Ralph Templeton still owned this land and he'd get those houses built if it was the last thing he did. He shivered in the cold morning air and turned for home. Next, the telephone call that would bring the men and the lorries to clear the grass of the rubbish and then fill the entrance with soil carried away from the road works the other side of Culworth. He clenched his fist and punched the air. He'd win, see if he didn't.

He watched all morning while the men cleared up. Two lorry loads of rubbish, they collected. They found some more boards and replaced the ones the travellers had pulled down from the chapel. By lunchtime the whole site was clear, and by mid afternoon the soil had been tipped to secure the entrance.

Muriel was waiting for him when he got home. 'Are you all right, dear? I've been so worried about you.'

'I've only been watching, not doing anything, but I am tired.'

'I'll make a sandwich for you, you've had a long day. Sit down and rest. By the way Ralph, there's been a telephone call from a man called Colonel something or another, I couldn't catch his name, but he's chairman of the County Council and he says he thinks he went to school with you. He's ringing back in about an hour.'

'I wonder who that is?'

The telephone call came while Muriel was out with Pericles. When she returned Ralph flung his arms round her and danced her round the hall.

'Muriel, Muriel, that was Nobby Winterton-Clark on the phone, he rang us several times that Sunday when we went out for the day. He's been on holiday since then and just got back. Remembers me from prep school, we shared the same dorm and were in the cricket team together. He's heard about my intention of having houses to rent, realised who I must be, and he's weighing in on my side, by putting in some good spade work before the planning meeting this week. He wants to make sure my new application goes through. Delighted to be of service, very concerned about the drain of people from the villages hereabouts, and hopes my plans will bear fruit in other places too. Isn't that marvellous?'

'Oh, Ralph, how lovely, I'm so pleased.' Muriel clapped her hands with glee. 'We really will have Hipkin Gardens then?'

'Yes, fingers crossed we will. We'll go out for dinner tonight. Not the George, we'll try that new place, the other side of Penny Fawcett. I'll book the table right now. Everything's turning out right, isn't it?'

'Oh Ralph, I'm so pleased, you've just no idea. You see, the village will like what we're doing won't they? Just eight houses is absolutely right, isn't it?'

She wore her claret-coloured dress with the low neckline and swirling skirt, Ralph his newest suit, light grey with the finest white pin stripe. He looked so handsome, she was so proud of him. Her heart wept a little, wishing he had sons to follow on. He would have made a lovely father and his children would have been so good-looking. No more Templetons. No more at all. It was all very sad. Then it occurred to her there were Templetons of a kind, living and working on the land still. Templeton land. A germ of an idea came to her, but then they arrived at the hotel and

Ralph was opening her door for her, and out of habit she braced herself for facing a new place. She took strength from the reassuring feel of Ralph's hand on her elbow guiding her up the steps. With him there there was nothing to fear, it wasn't like it used to be. Now she had Ralph to keep her safe.

Ralph dropped her off at the front door while he took the car round by Pipe and Nook Lane to put it away in the garage. How odd, Pericles always ran to greet her. She went to his basket in the kitchen. He lay quite still, his eyes glazed. 'Pericles? Are you all right, dear?' His breathing was unsteady and kind of ragged, his tail wagged very slightly, and he tried to lick her hand as she patted him and then there was a long shuddering sigh.

Muriel knelt down by his basket and laid her hand on his flank. There was only a very slight movement of his chest as he breathed, and then even that stopped.

'Oh Pericles, oh no, oh no!' Her tears dropped onto his head and she gently wiped them away. Her dear good friend, who'd been through thick and thin with her, troubles and joys, and now he was gone. His bright red collar, and his bright red lead. She'd loved them. They'd made him look so smart. Her hand hovered above his head for a moment and then she stroked him right from the tip of his nose to the root of his tail. Once, twice, three times. 'Goodbye Pericles. Goodbye.'

She heard Ralph's footsteps coming up the garden path.

'Muriel, I've been thinking . . . why, my dear, what's happened?' Muriel pointed mutely to the basket. Ralph looked at the old dog, lying as though he was still sleeping. He knelt down to lay his hand on Pericles' ribs. There was an unwelcome stillness. 'Oh, Muriel, I'm so sorry. Come here.' He helped her to stand up and Ralph folded her in his arms and hugged her closely to him. 'Never forget, my dear, he had the loveliest life and the loveliest mistress any dog has any right to expect. He wanted for nothing, and he's gone before life became too much of a burden, and for that we must be grateful.'

Muriel sobbed onto Ralph's new suit. 'I bought him because I needed someone to love and someone to love me. And he did, he did, he loved me. Now he's gone.'

'Will I make a good understudy?' Ralph held her away from his chest and smiled at her. She lifted her eyes and smiled back, 'Oh yes, you will, you will. No dog could match you, but it doesn't mean I shan't miss him at every turn.'

'Of course you will, my dear, and if you really want we could always . . . No, I'll save that for another day. Don't you think it was splendid that you were here when he went? He must have waited for you to come home and then let go. Tomorrow, I shall dig a deep, deep, hole at the end of the garden by the cherry tree, and we'll bury him there and then I shall go to the stonemason's and get a simple block of stone and we'll have whatever words you want engraved on it. That way he'll always be sleeping close at hand in your garden. Never far away.'

'Oh Ralph, what a lovely idea. Just "Pericles, a dear friend." Could we get a blanket and cover him, please?'

'Of course.'

It was Neville Neal who rang to tell Ralph that the planning committee had passed his application by a majority of one.

'How did you manage to persuade them to say yes? Not having taken my advice, I fully expected they'd all say "No" yet again.'

'Simply a very good idea they couldn't allow to be dismissed. And it is a good idea, and I'm very grateful for all the help you gave me. We can't wait to get going with the actual building now.'

'I did mention it before, Sir Ralph, but you didn't take me up on it, should you be in need of some capital, I would be more than interested to be of use in that sphere.'

'Thank you, but no. That won't be necessary.'

'I see, well, should circumstances change, then ring me any time, I shall be very willing to listen to any proposal.'

'Thank you again Neville, best wishes to you and Liz.' Ralph put down the receiver and shouted 'MURIEL!'

'Yes, I'm coming.' She appeared in the study doorway wearing a white nightgown. Her feet were bare, her hair brushed and hanging loose, and for a brief moment Ralph saw the girl he'd known all those years ago, the one he'd kissed over the little gate at the back of the churchyard; he on one side, she the other, the shy youthful gesture of two young things who'd thought they would never see each other ever again. The finality of their parting had lain like a stone in his heart for months.

'Muriel, my dear.' He held out his arms and she ran into them and he hugged her tightly. 'We've won, we've won, you and I, we've won.' He kissed her hard, and she kissed him back. 'My dear, that was Neville. The meeting's just finished and they've granted permission. Eight houses. Hipkin Gardens can go ahead.'

'Champagne! I'll get it.'

'Certainly not, I shall, that's my prerogative, Lady Templeton.'

They stood together in their sitting room and toasted the success of their venture. 'To the Templetons, long may they reign in Turnham Malpas!'

Chapter 19

Jimbo had been asked to cater for twelve guests at Mr
Fitch's dinner party. In the event on the night two people,
friends of Mr Fitch, had telephoned to say their car had been
involved in a multiple pile up on the Culworth bypass, and
although not seriously hurt in any way, they were badly
shaken and were returning home. So, gathered in the
drawing room of Mr Fitch's private flat were Peter and
Caroline, Muriel and Ralph, Harriet and Jimbo, Sir Ronald
and Lady Bissett, and Craddock Fitch and someone called
Oriana Duncan-Lewis whom he introduced, with a slight
hesitation, as a family friend. She was a small, slender
woman in her fifties, elegantly dressed; carefully made-up
face, socially very assured, with an effusive manner which
didn't quite ring true. Mr Fitch took her round introducing
everybody.

'Delighted to meet you, Jimbo. Craddock has told me so
much about you. You and your wonderful food. I'm
looking forward to sampling it tonight. This must be your
wife. You must be awfully proud of your husband, he's
doing a wonderful job here. He's lucky to have someone
like you to look after his domestic matters while he fights

the battles out in the market place, isn't he? Behind every great man et cetera. You have children, Harriet, my dear?'

Harriet, seething at the implication that all she was fit for was giving birth and doing the washing up, replied through gritted teeth. 'Four.'

'Four? Then you'll be glad of the opportunity for an evening out, I'm sure. I expect you don't get many opportunities to socialise.' She swept on to Caroline.

'And you're . . . '

'Dr Caroline Harris.'

'You're a career woman, then.'

'You could say so. This is my husband, Peter Harris.' Oriana melted at the sight of Peter. From her five-feet-nothing height she looked up at him, with deep appreciation in her eyes. 'Considering how far out in the sticks this place is, there are some remarkably attractive people living here. First Jimbo and now you. Craddock, you didn't tell me how utterly delightful I should find your guests to be. And you, you must be Sir Ralph. Good evening, and good evening to you, Lady Templeton.' The two of them shook hands with her but from where Jimbo was standing he could see that neither Muriel nor Ralph relished the meeting. 'It must be terrible for you to come here and see this place when it was once your home, Ralph. You have my every sympathy.' She beamed understandingly at him, and patted his arm.

'It is a matter of indifference to me, in fact. I've created a whole new lifestyle for myself and my wife. and really wouldn't enjoy the burden of such a large property as this.' He curtly nodded his head to her and turned away to speak to Peter. Muriel was left to bear the brunt.

'I'm sure Craddock would be delighted to show you round.'

'That's most kind, but no thank you. Not when Ralph's not interested.'

They talked for five more minutes and then Mr Fitch asked everyone to go into dinner. The dining table was round, and beautifully set with crystal and china and a silver candelabra, in the centre a small flower arrangement in subtle shades of green and white. The wall lights threw an apricot glow over the table, enhancing its appeal and setting the crystal and silver twinkling. Muriel was fearful of being placed next to Mr Fitch, and in fact as senior lady guest that was exactly where she was led. A suave, well experienced host, Mr Fitch soon had everyone seated: Oriana on the other side of him, Jimbo next to her, with Caroline on his other side, then Ralph, then Harriet, then Sir Ronald, then Lady Bissett, and next to her Peter made the tenth person. Muriel was so pleased to have Peter on her other side, at least he would help to keep the conversation going. She sat back slightly so that Peter and Mr Fitch had an uninter-rupted view of each other.

'Before we commence eating would you be so kind as to say Grace, Rector?'

Peter bowed his head and said, 'Ever mindful of your bounteous gifts to us, oh Lord, we thank you for the food we are about to eat. Amen.'

During the meal the conversation waxed and waned. Mr Fitch did his best to put Muriel at ease by asking her about village life before she and her parents had left all those years ago.

'Oh yes, Mr Fitch, every November there was this enormous bonfire up here. On Home Farm field. Ralph's father had the estate workers collecting the wood for it for weeks before. He always made sure he was at home for Guy Fawkes night. We always had a guy to burn, and potatoes in their jackets cooked in the big cooking range, and then when the children were going home they were each given a toffee apple. The grown-ups had cider and ale to drink and it all got very merry.' Her eyes were alight with the joy of recollecting those happy celebrations of so many years ago. Ralph watched her and was saddened by her memories. Mr Fitch encouraged her to reminisce; Jimbo could see his mind storing all this innocently given information.

'Then in the summer there was always the Village Fair. That took weeks to get ready for. That was held on Home Farm field too. Ralph's father paid for roundabouts for the children, we had coconut shies, and guess the weight of the fat lady, wrestling matches, though my mother would never let me watch those, there were cakestalls and craft stalls run by the ladies from the church. Tugs of war between teams from the Jug and Bottle in Penny Fawcett and our own Royal Oak. The Big House cook made lots of food for us to eat, the Morris dancers came from Penny Fawcett, and then in the early evening there was dancing to a band. They were good times. Of course we still have Stocks Day. Even during the war we always held Stocks Day.'

'Stocks Day?' Mr Fitch offered her more wine. 'What is this Stocks Day?'

Muriel rambled on with Mr Fitch listening intently. Jimbo's heart began to sink. He suddenly realised what was going on in the razor-sharp brain of Craddock Fitch. A takeover bid, no less.

'Of course, Jimbo here does a firework display for us now, don't you Jimbo?'

He nodded, and Mr Fitch said, 'Charter-Plackett! I'd no idea you were a pyrotechnic expert?'

Before he could answer Sheila Bissett interrupted. 'Oh

yes, Mr Fitch, he's marvellous at it. When Sir Ralph and Lady Templeton married he did a wonderful finale with catherine wheels in the shape of their initials. It was brilliant, wasn't it, Sir Ralph?'

'Absolutely.'

'Are firework displays a hobby of yours, then?'

Jimbo agreed they were. Muriel remarked, 'And I'd forgotten the children from the school always did a PT display on the day of the Village Fair, and my husband's father always presented each of them with a small gift for being so clever. One year I got a mouth organ, I loved it, but the noise I made annoyed mother and I had to put it away in a drawer. I have it somewhere. Yes, definitely somewhere. Small things mean so much to a child, don't they?' Muriel realised she was verging on the ridiculous in such sophisticated company. She blushed and fell silent.

Sheila Bissett filled the silence with, 'Wouldn't it be lovely if we had a Village Fair and a bonfire now? Don't you think so, Sir Ralph? You'll have to give it some thought, Mr Fitch. Don't you think, Sir Ralph?'

Ralph dabbed his mouth with his napkin and said, 'Ask Mr Fitch.'

So Sheila did.

'I had been thinking on those lines myself. Of course, I'd need someone to advise me on how to go about it, someone who remembers.' He looked questioningly at Muriel, eyebrows raised, face full of anticipation. She looked up and was about to nod her head in agreement when she caught Jimbo's eye. He quickly signalled a warning to her, and she glanced across the table at Ralph before replying. She had seen him angry before but never like this. It flashed through her mind how she'd persuaded him to come against his better judgement, and she saw clear as light the trap into which she'd fallen. Knives and forks were still. Jaws stopped. Wine untouched. Only Sheila Bissett moved; she was draining the last dregs of her wine. When she put down her glass she looked around the table.

'You'd be glad to help wouldn't you, Sir Ralph too? You both remember, don't you?'

Ralph put his napkin down beside his empty plate. In a voice full of barely controlled anger, he replied, 'I'm afraid Muriel and I will be too busy supervising the building of our houses in Hipkin Gardens to be free to act in any kind of an advisory capacity to anything at all. The houses will take priority over any other pettifogging concerns.'

Mr Fitch allowed a small smile to hover on his lips. 'How very disappointing. You've got permission to build then?'

'Yes, we have.'

'I'd be delighted to see your plans. I trained as an architect, a highly desirable qualification for the chairman of a major building company, is it not?' He smiled at Muriel inviting her approval, but she didn't look up. 'We don't want the village spoilt in any way, do we, Rector? You must have a specially close interest in these houses.'

Peter, anxious to defuse the overwrought atmosphere, assured Mr Fitch that Sir Ralph always had the interests of the village at heart and he was absolutely confident that the houses would be built in very good taste. Sheila, having got the bit between her teeth, wouldn't let the matter of the Fair and bonfire rest.

'How about it then, Mr Fitch? Can we look forward to a bonfire night this year? There's still time.'

'I think it would be absolutely perfect to have a Village Fair here and reinstate the bonfire night. Charter-Plackett, you have the kitchens and the staff, you would cater for it, wouldn't you? And I'd want a firework display to round off the evening.'

Jimbo, thinking on his feet, knew he'd no alternative but to agree and at the same time wondered how his relationship with Ralph would suffer. Before he could reply, Oriana gazing adoringly at Mr Fitch said, 'Oh, Craddock, could I be the one to light the bonfire?'

Muriel, without pausing for thought, said decisively, 'Oh no, I'm sorry, Ralph would have to do that, it's always a Templeton who lights the bonfire.'

It was only Ralph's innate good manners which prevented him from making a biting riposte to Muriel's announcement. Humiliation sat badly on his shoulders, and that was just how it felt. Total humiliation at the hands of this — this upstart. Under his eyebrows he shot an angry glance at Mr Fitch, and then said smoothly, 'I'm quite sure that Mrs Duncan-Lewis would make a much more decorative igniter of the bonfire than myself, and I shall gladly relinquish my time-honoured post to allow her to perform the ceremony.' He raised his glass in salute to her. Jimbo mentally applauded Ralph's adroit escape.

The situation was rescued by the waiters coming to clear away the dishes and serve the pudding. This provided a welcome break and the conversation broke up. Peter began discussing Trades Union business with Ron, Sheila leant across to speak to Caroline about the twins, and Ralph and Harriet began a discussion about the level of trade in the Store. Mr Fitch and Oriana discussed the best method for lighting bonfires, leaving Muriel and Jimbo talking about Flick and her two cats. When the pudding was cleared away Mr Fitch suggested sampling the cheeseboard, but his guests declined so they retired to the drawing room for coffee.

Sadie chose to bring it in, sensing that for the waiters, serving at table was one thing but serving people seated in armchairs and sofas would be too much of a challenge. Unruffled and looking elegant in a black tailored suit, she began pouring coffee. Only Sheila Bissett made a fuss. 'Sadie! how kind of you to be helping out. I didn't realise you were slaving away in the kitchen on our behalf.'

'All part of the Charter-Plackett service, Lady Bissett.' She served Oriana and then Mr Fitch. He looked up at her to say thank you, and stopped in his tracks.

'Why, you're . . .? Isn't it? It is. It's Sadie Chandler, isn't it?' Sadie put down the coffee pot, handed him the cream and then said, 'Well, yes I was Sadie Chandler but . . . oh! my word! You're not? No, you can't be. Yes, you are. Surely you're *Henry* Fitch. Aren't you?'

Mr Fitch stood up, put down his coffee cup, took her by the forearms and kissed her on both cheeks. 'You knew me as Henry, but I've used my other name for years.'

'Isn't this amazing. How long is it since . . . '

'I don't think we'll go into that. Let's say it's a long time since we met. How do you come to be here?'

'I have the honour to be Ji . . . Mr Charter-Plackett's mother-in-law.'

'My word! As they say, what a small world. I really can't believe we've met up again after all this time. What a coincidence. Oriana, may I introduce Sadie Chandler, of course that's not your name now, is it?'

'No, I'm Sadie Beauchamp now.'

'Introduce Sadie Beauchamp. We knew each other in our teens. Sadie this is Oriana Duncan-Lewis, a friend of the family.' Oriana shook hands with Sadie, in the manner of one unaccustomed to shaking hands with a minion. 'Charmed, I'm sure,' she murmured.

'I must finish serving coffee. I don't normally do this, but Jimbo wouldn't have enjoyed himself if he was fretting about the food, so I volunteered to step in.'

'We'll talk later, shall we? We mustn't bore my guests recalling past times. Would you join us?'

'Love to! What fun! I'll get myself a cup.'

Ralph's Mercedes roared down the drive just before midnight. Muriel sat miserably beside him, torn to shreds by remorse. If only she could put back the clock. Not just to seven o'clock that evening, but about three years. Then she would be living in her neat little Glebe Cottage, with her dear Pericles, with her dear little garden wearing its autumn clothes and absolutely no problems of any kind at all. She'd be sitting at the till in Harriet's tea room with nothing more challenging than handing out menus and taking money. She'd be lonely and life would be dull, but how blessedly unruffled compared with now. It wasn't that she regretted marrying Ralph, it was just that she knew she'd inadvertently roasted him on a spit tonight at the dinner. Not only roasted him but served him up, trussed, on a plate for Mr Fitch's consumption. She owed him a hugely enormous apology, but the right words wouldn't come. What was worse, Ralph wasn't even speaking to her.

She peeped at his profile as they surged through the gates. He looked grim. Yes, that best described him. Grim. Heaven alone knew how she would make amends. As they passed the church he spoke.

'My dear. Am I forgiven?'

Startled, Muriel said, 'Forgiven?'

'Yes. I have behaved like a complete boor this evening, all I can hope is that you will accept my apology.'

'Your apology! Ralph, it's myself who should be

apologising. I let my tongue run away with me without a single thought for how you must have been feeling. I shall never forgive myself.'

He pulled up outside their garage, turned off the engine and switched on the courtesy light. He sat gripping the steering wheel. 'No, Muriel, you're not at fault. Not at all. You are so straightforward, you haven't a devious bone in your body, so you can't be blamed for becoming embroiled by a cunning swin . . . cunning specimen like Fitch. It was for me to have dealt with the situation much sooner than I did. My fault lay in allowing my pride to overcome my common sense. There is no way that I could possibly buy back and maintain a property of such a size as Turnham House. I wouldn't want to anyway, there wouldn't be any point. But it bites right into my innermost soul to see a monied upstart like Craddock Fitch lording it up there, in my father's house, where I grew up. I came close to walking out. But that would have been a betrayal of all my family have stood for. A betrayal of good breeding. Something Craddock Fitch, with all his money, will never have. I've sorted my feelings out now, and accepted the position.'

'Oh Ralph!' He put his arm along the back of her seat and bent his head to kiss her. Full of gratitude for the generosity of his spirit in not blaming her for what had happened, she turned to face him and as he kissed her she experienced an uncontrollable surge of passion. And Ralph rejoiced that his patient loving of her had at last reaped this rich reward for them both.

A few minutes later Peter and Caroline drove past up Pipe and Nook Lane to their garage. They both stared straight ahead, not wishing to embarrass the occupants of the Mercedes.

'Well, really! And illuminated too!'

'Caroline!'

'You're being stuffy again, Peter Harris. I keep telling you about it. Let's be glad they're all right with each other. I feared they would have a row to end all rows, because she really did put her foot in it.'

Chapter 20

Sadie was late the following morning. There was a stack of mail orders to be attended to, and Jimbo was wanting to get them ready for the twelve o'clock post. If she didn't turn up soon he'd have to ask Harriet to come in to help. Then he remembered: of course it was Saturday and the children were at home. Damn and blast. Where was the woman?'

At a quarter to ten Sadie arrived. 'Don't look at me like that. You're privileged I work on Saturday mornings at all.'

'My God, Sadie, you look terrible.'

'Thank you. That's a very unkind and thoughtless remark to make.'

'You do, though. Hell's bells.'

'Lack of sleep. It was four o'clock before I got to bed.'

'Four o'clock?'

'Yes. Craddock and I sat up till half past three talking. I realise now I'm much too old for such juvenile capers.'

'May I ask how you come to know him?'

'We knew each other in our teens. In a fit of pique, I threw him over for Harriet's father. Had I had an old head on my young shoulders, I would have given her father the order of the boot and married Craddock instead.'

'Wow! He obviously isn't married now.'

'Oh, he was, but it's a long, very sad story. If I tell you, you mustn't tell anyone else, please? Promise?'

Jimbo drew a finger across his throat. 'Cut my throat and hope to die.'

'He told me that within three months of me finishing with him he met and married someone called Annette. He was just twenty and she was eighteen. They had four very happy years together and produced two sons. Apparently Henry, or rather, Craddock, felt that the two boys were his crowning achievement. He positively gloried in them. *Unfortunately*, dear Annette met this dashing army major and before you could say knife he resigned his commission and she hopped off to South America with him, where he became something big in polo. Consequently Craddock has not seen his boys since then. It's a continuous throbbing pain for him, and gets no better as the years go by. So he's thrown himself into his work. So now you know, Jimbo dear, and not a word to anyone. Busy, busy. Must get on. Coffee please. Black!'

He'd just returned from delivering Sadie's coffee when Pat Duckett came in. She wandered round the shelves putting a few items into her wire basket and frequently glancing at him. Eventually she came to the meat counter where he was topping up the display of joints of beef.

'Jimbo, could you give me some advice?'

'Of course, if I can. Willingly. Fire away.'

'This letter came through my door this morning. I 'aven't told Dad, but it's to do with him really, but I'm not going to say anything to 'im till I've decided what I want to do. Read it and see what you think.'

The letter was from Craddock Fitch, suggesting that Pat and her father go to live in the old Head Gardener's House at

Turnham House, and her father could be in charge of the gardens on a permanent basis. He realised this would give her the problem of what to do with her cottage, but he would be more than willing to purchase it from her at its proper market value. Would she like to take time to consider the matter.

Jimbo folded up the letter when he'd read it and replaced it in the envelope.

'Well, what shall I do?'

'My word, Pat, it's a big decision and no mistake. First, does your Dad want to be up there permanently?'

'Oh yes, he loves it. He's got all sorts of plans and he's itching to get cracking. Worked like a slave since he started and Jeremy's delighted with him. I 'ave 'eard the house has been done up something wonderful, all new fully-fitted kitchen and bathroom and that and painted throughout, and there's even a downstairs lav. Apparently it's 'ardly had anything done to it since Muriel's father left, so yer can imagine, Gawd 'elp us, it was a tip. Four bedrooms, there is. Imagine that. We'd all have one each. And Barry's mother says central heating too. Her Barry fitted the kitchen so she knows all about it. Bliss. Total bliss. Course we'd need new furniture. My stuff's rubbish. But then I'd have the money to buy it, wouldn't I? And there's Dad's redundancy money as well. It's bloomin' tempting, believe me.'

Jimmy Glover came to the counter to choose his meat for the weekend.

'You two plotting something, are yer?'

Pat shook her head. 'No, no, just 'aving a business consultation.'

'Spect it's about whether you're going to accept old Fitch's offer.'

'What offer?'

'That offer to buy your cottage. His typist was telling me about it last night when I took her to the station.'

'She'd no business discussing my private affairs with you, Jimmy Glover.'

'Great friends we are. She's bought this car and it's never been right since the day she got it, always in for something or another, and I've got to know her really well with keeping on giving her lifts. Any news I want to know about up there she tells me. It doesn't take much to egg her on to reveal all.'

'Well, honestly. What a cheek.'

'So you're taking it up, are yer?'

'Mind yer own business!'

'Yer'll be a traitor if yer take him up on 'is offer.'

'Traitor? Don't you call me a traitor, Jimmy Glover. You're rare an' glad to ferry people back and forth to Culworth Station in your taxi, I've noticed. You don't call that being a traitor, then?'

Jimbo intervened. 'In purely hard cash terms, it would be a good bargain for Pat. She could invest the money and have a nice little nest egg growing against the time when her father retired. Think about it over the weekend, Pat, and we'll have another talk on Monday. Yours truly would be glad to help with investments if you would like me to.'

Jimmy chose a pork chop and half a pound of braising steak. 'Tell yer what, yer'd need a bike. Kill yer, running up and down that drive to the school three times a day.'

Pat laughed. 'It'ud be worth it! Can yer imagine, a whole big beautiful house for us. If our Dean gets to university, I wouldn't mind 'is friends coming to a house like that. I couldn't ask 'em to my old cottage. Oh! no! Things are looking up for me, aren't they Jimbo?'

Jimbo studied her face before replying. He'd known her something like five years now, and he'd never seen her looking so joyous. Years had rolled from her face, the deep lines between her eyebrows and her downturned mouth were gone. Her dark eyes were sparkling bright and for the first time in a long while she looked her age. She deserved good luck. She'd earned it.

'They certainly are. And I'm glad. Must press on. Lots to do. Come in Monday after you've talked to the noble parent. We'll have another discussion.'

Pat gave him the thumbs-up sign and said to Jimmy, 'And you keep your trap shut about this. You've 'ad plenty of luck with your big win, this time it's my turn.' She spun on her heel and headed for the till.

Jimbo reflected that this was another move in Craddock Fitch's master plan. He hoped Ralph would be astute enough to accept what he couldn't change and still manage to maintain his place as the benevolent figurehead of the village.

Later that same day Ralph and Muriel were making the best of the autumn days by drinking their afternoon tea in the garden. The sun came round at just the right angle at this time of year and made a lovely pool of sunlight around four o'clock by their garden table and chairs.

'A biscuit, Ralph?'

'No, thank you dear, you have one though.'

'Yes, I will. Do you remember how Pericles used to love a corner of my biscuit?'

'Yes, or the whole biscuit given half a chance! Have you thought about getting a replacement for Peric . . . ' They became aware of shouting out in the lane.

Muriel said, 'What's that? Who's shouting?'

'I don't know. I'll go take a look.' Muriel sat enjoying the sun and planning the end-of-season gardening jobs she would begin once her tea was finished. She closed her eyes and lifted her face to the sun. She could still hear shouting and a curious chanting noise and when Ralph didn't return, she went in search of him.

He was opening the front door when she entered the hall. Through the open door she could see banners. She called anxiously, 'What's happening, dear? What is it?'

Ralph stood four-square on the stone step. Facing him was Arthur Prior, holding a banner. Behind him was an assortment of villagers mostly holding banners, all of them chanting. The banners read:

'NO MORE HOUSES IN TURNHAM MALPAS'
'GREED! GREED! GREED!'
'WE SHALL APPEAL'
'OUT! OUT! OUT!'
'WE SHALL OVERCOME'

Beyond the crowd were the onlookers, some watching gleefully, others apprehensively. Ralph, so boiling with anger he could recognise no one but Arthur, thought, Well I've won, so it's all a waste of time. The fools. He waited for the shouting to stop and then, addressing Arthur, said quietly: 'Kindly remove yourself and your band of followers from outside my house.'

'Public road, can stand where we like.'

'You're causing a public nuisance.'

'Who says?'

'I do.'

'Oh, well,' Arthur said, 'in that case we'd better listen.' He turned to the crowd behind him and shouted, 'The Lord of the Manor has spoken, doff your caps everyone, *Sir*

Ralph has spoken.' He took off his corduroy cap and stood humbly holding it in his hands, head inclined in submission.

Raising his head slightly and looking at Ralph somewhere at the level of his top waistcoat button, Arthur said, 'We're not going to let this go through. We intend to appeal.'

'Appeal all you like. What's done's done and you won't alter it. Eight houses for rent in a village this size is just right. Your sons won't need them but there are plenty of villagers who will.'

'And what about *your* sons? Will they be needing a house to rent?'

The crowd tittered. Ralph stared silently at Arthur. The demonstrators began tapping the ends of their banners on the ground, tauntingly keeping time with their chanting. Arthur waited on a reply.

'There's no more to say. The houses will be built and there's an end to the matter.'

Arthur raised his banner and shook it in time with the chant. 'GREED! GREED! GREED! MONEY! MONEY! MONEY!'

Some of the spectators joined the ranks of the protesters and swelled the shouting. Others, like Alan Crimble and Georgie, simply observed.

Georgie nudged Alan and whispered, 'There's going to be a fight!'

'No, not them, two old geysers like them's not going to fight.'

Alan stood on tiptoe and saw Ralph take a step forward. Arthur, mistaking his intentions, raised the banner in self defence. Ralph stepped back and stumbled against the edge of the stone step. The colour of his face changed instantly to a deathly grey, his hand went to his chest, and then he clawed at his throat as though trying to undo his collar to get more air. Beads of sweat appeared on his face and it went even more grey. The crowd fell silent. Muriel, who was still standing in the hall, and trembling from head to foot, didn't realise that Ralph was ill and it was only when he began to crumple to the ground that she let out a screech of terror. 'Ralph! Ralph!'

He fell partly on the road, partly on the stone step, his head missing the boot scraper by inches. Muriel rushed to his side, loosened his tie and undid the top button of his collar; she shook him and shouted his name over and over again, but he remained silent, his grey, grey face glistening with sweat. 'Do something, do something for him, please, please,' she pleaded. In a harsh whisper Alan said, 'God, Georgie, he's had a heart attack!'

'Do something! Alan! do something! Go on, you know what to do. That massage and breathing. Go on!'

'I can't, I'm scared.'

'Go on, it might be too late if you don't.'

Alan pushed his way through the crowd and shouted, 'Get an ambulance, go on, get an ambulance, someone get Dr Harris!' He roughly pushed Muriel out of the way and knelt down beside Ralph. He felt his neck where he knew the pulse would beat most strongly and, finding no pulse, began chest massage. One, two, three, four, five, then tilting back Ralph's head he pinched his nose and bent down to blow into his mouth. Then both hands to pump his chest. One two three four five. Then blow, blow, blow, blow, blow. Someone said 'There's no one in at the rectory,' and Alan thought 'Hell's bells, it's up to me.' The only movement was him working on Ralph. The crowd was silent and afraid. Muriel stood on the step weeping uncontrollably. Georgie, inspired by Alan's competent manner, went to comfort Muriel.

In a shocked, quiet voice Arthur said, 'God help us, is he breathing?'

'Not yet.' Alan continued working on him. After one more try he stopped and checked his pulse. 'He's got going again.' A rustle of relief ran around the crowd, now swelled to twice it's size with people who'd come out in surprise at the sudden silence and were standing on tiptoe at the back trying to see what had happened. Those who'd been demonstrating quietly put their banners out of sight.

Someone had brought out a blanket and Alan covered Ralph with it and stayed kneeling beside him, monitoring his pulse. Someone else brought a brandy for Muriel, and Arthur got a kitchen chair out of her house so she could sit down.

'I never meant this to happen, Muriel.' Arthur pleaded with her for forgiveness. She ignored him and kept her eyes on Ralph.

Alan, on his knees beside Ralph; waited desperately for the ambulance to arrive, constantly checking him, and worried sick that he shouldn't die, at least until the ambulance arrived. He'd never prayed in all his life, but he did at that moment. The ambulance came. His prayers had been answered, Ralph was still breathing.

Muriel went with Ralph in the ambulance and as soon as it had moved off with its light flashing, Alan felt a tremendous surge of relief and his legs went to jelly and he felt sick. Georgie flung her arms round his neck and kissed him in front of the whole crowd.

'Wonderful, Alan, you were wonderful! If it hadn't been for you he would have been a goner.'

'Thank goodness you were there, Alan!'

'Where did you learn what to do?'

Alan laughed shakily. 'Watched it on telly.'

'Brilliant. Brilliant. Drink on me tonight, Alan, see yer in there. Right?'

'Right! Thanks!'

'Poor Sir Ralph! Hope he'll be all right. What a thing to happen!'

'That Arthur Prior has a lot to answer for. Where is he?'

Arthur had gone home, ashamed and fearful at what his pigheadedness had caused. He'd left his car parked in the village and walked all the way. If Ralph died, he knew he'd never forgive himself.

That night Alan served in the bar again. Bryn had to put a stop to the number of drinks he was expected to consume. 'Can he accept the money and have it later? Do you mind? He's already had three drinks and he won't be able to stand soon,' Bryn suggested.

'Congratulations! Best day's work you've done in a long time.'

'You must be proud of him, Georgie. Really proud.'

'Oh we are. I knew he'd turn up trumps.' She kissed his cheek and gave him a hug. Alan blushed, unaccustomed to such adulation.

'I only did what I learned from the telly. Anyone could have done it. Watched "Casualty" and that. Just hope his ticker keeps going.'

One of the customers said, 'You're staying in the village, Alan, aren't you now?'

He grinned at Georgie. 'I hope so, but we'll see.'

Georgie agreed. 'Well, of course he is. I've always known what a good bloke he is, always. He's got to stay, hasn't he?'

'Certainly. How would you run this place without 'im?'

'Exactly!'

Standing at the bar was Linda from the Store. 'Gin and tonic, Alan, please, and get one for yourself.'

'Hello, we don't usually see you in here.'

'No, well, I had to come to see our hero, hadn't I?'

Alan blushed again. 'Don't know about that. I only did what anyone else would have done.'

'Well, I certainly couldn't have done it, could you Bryn?'

'No, not me.'

'Aren't you drinking with me, then?'

'Can I have the money instead? I've already had three, and that's more than enough when I'm working.'

'Yes, of course. Well, here's to you. Our hero of the hour.' Linda sipped her gin and then placed her glass down on the counter. She put the change Alan gave her in her purse and said, 'What's your night off this next week?'

'Monday.'

'I'll give my aerobics a miss then and buy you a drink.'

Alan straightened the knot in his tie, served another customer and then said, 'I'll take you up on that.'

'Pick you up then when I finish at the Store. Go into Culworth, you won't want to drink where you work.'

'No, that's right. I'll be ready.'

In the ambulance Ralph's heart had arrested for a second time, and the paramedics had to work hard to start him again. For twenty-four hours Muriel never left his side. On the second day Caroline took her home to take a bath and get clean clothes, but all the time she was intensely afraid that Ralph would slip away while she was in Turnham Malpas and he'd die alone. That was the one thing she couldn't bear, the thought that he might die alone.

When he'd been in hospital three days, wired to an

unimaginable complexity of machinery, he opened his eyes and recognised her. 'Why, Muriel, you're still here.' His voice, shaky and soft, sounded not one jot like the voice to which she was accustomed. All his vigour had gone, there was no strength left for teasing or anything else.

'Of course I am, Ralph. Where would you be if it was I who was ill? Right beside me holding my hand. My dear.' She stood up reaching round the wires kissed his forehead. 'I do love you, Ralph. You gave me such a scare.'

Ralph smiled gently and closed his eyes. After a few minutes he said, 'I can remember Alan, what was he doing?'

'Just helping you, dear. We were lucky he was there. He's sent you a card wishing you all the best. I've already written to him to thank him for what he did. When you're home we shall think of something we can do for him to show our gratitude.'

'I've forgotten what it was all about.'

'Well, never mind, you concentrate on getting well.'

Muriel held his hand to her cheek and sat watching him. How she loved him. Really loved him. Her life could be divided into two halves, the second half being the year and three-quarters she'd been married to Ralph. More had happened to her in that time than in all the rest of her life put together. He made her feel so safe, and yet life was so exciting. She could face almost anything knowing she had him with her. What would she do if he . . . No, she wasn't going to think about that. Be positive, that's right, be positive.

'Drink of water, please.'

'I'll get the nurse.'

After the nurse had settled him again and checked the dials and adjusted the bedclothes, she said, 'There's a visitor just come, do you feel able to see him, Sir Ralph?'

Muriel said, 'Oh that'll be the rector. Yes, do ask him to come in.'

But it wasn't Peter; it was Arthur Prior. He stood hesitantly in the doorway, waiting.

Muriel jumped up, surprised and alarmed.

'I don't think you should come in, if you don't mind.'

'Yes, I know, but I . . . '

Muriel put her hands on his chest and tried to push him out. 'I don't want him having another attack, he's not really stable yet. You can see all the wires and things, he's very ill. Please, please go away.'

'Yes, but I want to say . . . '

'You're going ahead with the appeal, is that it?'

'That wasn't what I was going to say, all I'm wanting . . . '

'Just please go away, I don't want you here.' Muriel stamped her foot and became very agitated. Ralph weakly called out, 'What is it, Arthur?'

He stepped back into the room. 'I can't sleep for the worry. I've come to say I shan't be making an appeal. I genuinely thought you would sell to make money out of it, but Neville Neal tells me you really do intend to build and rent. That's all right by me. I wouldn't want to cause a man's d– I wouldn't want to cause trouble and I'm very sorry you're so ill.'

'Thank you, we'll talk another time when I'm feeling better.'

'You intend coming round then?' Arthur said smiling.

'Oh yes, I've everything to live for.' He painstakingly felt about on the counterpane for Muriel's hand and when he'd found it he held it tightly.

'Well, I'm glad you're still going to be around. Can't keep a good man down, can you?'

'No, that's right.'

'I'll be off then.' Arthur nodded to Muriel, hesitated, and then said, 'I want things to be all right between us.' He nodded to Ralph and left the room.

'I feel ashamed of stamping my foot and getting annoyed.'

'I quite like you in a temper, it suits you.'

'Ralph! Go to sleep! I'll stay with you and then while you sleep, I'll use your telephone and tell Caroline how much you've improved. You must have, if you're starting to tease.'

Some two weeks later, when Muriel popped home for some fresh clothes for Ralph, she checked the messages on the answerphone and found a call on it from the architect, asking to come to see them with the final plans for Hipkin Gardens. Muriel knew how pleased Ralph would be, but he wouldn't be able to be there, she'd have to put the architect off till Ralph was better. Yes, that's what she'd do, tell Ralph and then put him off. He needed to be there to walk round the site and crystallise their thoughts, yes and that would be weeks yet. Yes, she'd postpone his visit. Now Ralph was no longer connected to all the wires and pipes and could sit in a chair in his clothes he really did seem to be making progress, but he was by no means capable of dealing with business matters, not yet.

'When do you say he wants to come?'

'Next Wednesday.'

'And today's . . . '

'Friday.'

'Right. Don't put him off, we'll let him come.'

'Oh Ralph, I'm much braver than I was, but I really don't think I could talk to him, what if I get it all wrong, and you don't like it and he does the plans and then . . .'

'Don't worry my dear, I shall be there, I'll deal with it.'

She jumped to her feet, her hands clasped under her chin. 'You're not coming home, Ralph, you're not ready yet, not by any means. You're teasing, aren't you, teasing?'

'Never been more serious. I've had enough of this place. I'm discharging myself.'

'You can't, I won't let you.'

Ralph chuckled. 'That temper of yours is getting the better of you, my dear.'

'I shall ring for a nurse. They'll make you see sense.'

'They can't keep me here against my will.'

'I can.'

'Not even you can, Muriel. I've made up my mind I'm going home. I want to sit in front of the fire, and eat scones and drink tea with my wife. Go to bed in a proper bed with my wife beside me holding my hand. There's no better tonic, believe me.'

'I shan't make any scones and I shan't hold your hand, so you might as well stay here.'

'Come here to me.' She went closer to his chair. 'Closer. That's it. Now give me a kiss. A lovely long lingering kiss, and *then* tell me I can't go home.' Ralph's arms around her shoulders and her arms tucked between his back and the cushions, they kissed one of those deep satisfying kisses which say so much more than words. 'Oh Ralph, yes, please come home!'

They were disturbed by a polite cough. Muriel straightened up to find Peter waiting in the doorway.

'Shall I come back later?' His eyes were twinkling. 'I can if you wish, I have got someone else to see.'

Muriel blushed, and held her hands to her hot cheeks. Ralph beckoned to Peter. 'Come in, you're just the man I want to see. My wife is insisting that I go home . . . '

'I am not, it was your idea. Really it was, it was Ralph's. He's going to discharge himself. He shouldn't, should he?'

Peter gravely considered her question. 'No, he shouldn't, but being at home is a marvellous pick-me-up, I must admit, and he would get every care wouldn't he?'

'Oh yes, of course he would, but I . . . '

Ralph interrupted decisively. 'It's settled then. Muriel, ring for the nurse. Peter, give me an hour, I've got to see the consultant and persuade him I'm doing the right thing, I've got to pack and pay my bills, and then could you drive me home, if you're going straight back?'

'Certainly. An hour then.'

Ralph, resting his hands on the arms of his chair, had heaved himself upright before Peter had left the room. 'Now Muriel . . . '

They talked that evening sitting in front of the fire, drinking tea and eating scones.

'I like to sit in the firelight, you know, it smoothes out all my wrinkles and I can imagine I'm young again. More tea, dear?'

'Yes, please, and another scone.' When Muriel had placed his scone on his plate and made sure his tea was to hand, he asked her to listen to what he had to say.

'I have something to talk to you about and then we shall never, never mention it again. Not ever mention it again. I spoke to the consultant, as you know, and to sum up what he said, if I sit in a chair and do nothing, and be pernickety about my diet, and turn myself into a doddery old fool, then I might last ten years. But, Muriel, I don't want to be a foolish old man. I would much rather have five years living a full life than ten years watching TV and doing the crossword to pass the time. I know it's a difficult decision to make and we've never talked about it because we didn't know we would have it to face, but I wondered how *you* felt about the situation?'

Muriel picked up her cup and drank some of her tea while she found the right words to say. Then she answered him.

'Well, I certainly don't want to be married to a doddery old man. I love you as you are and I'm sure you would get quite miserable with nothing to do, then we'd get on each other's nerves and it wouldn't be lovely any more. So I'll watch over you and get advice from Caroline if I get stuck, and we'll try to carry on as if nothing has happened.'

He took her hand and said, 'Thank you, my dear, for being so understanding. Let's hope we shall have many more wonderful years together. The doctors have told me that I shall need regular checkups and will have to watch my diet and my weight and take sensible exercise, and they've given me a list of the foods I need to avoid. I know it will cause you a problem having to make a new approach to your shopping and cooking, and I'm sorry.'

'There's no need to be sorry, I shall be only too glad to help. And we *shall* have many more wonderful years together. First we've got to see the architect, and then you'll have to supervise the plans and make sure they're not skimping on anything, and then we shall need a holiday before they start building and . . . '

'You're turning into a martinet!'

'Oh, I shall be, don't worry. Enjoy that scone, because I don't think you'll be allowed many of those after today.'

'Help! The woman's a tyrant!'

When she'd cleared away their tea things, Muriel went into the garden in the dark to put the remaining two scones on her bird table, because she hated 'second day' scones. She stood by the cherry tree pretending to be looking at Pericles' headstone. With her back to the house, so Ralph couldn't possibly see, she wept painful scalding tears.

Chapter 21

Muriel had a list with her to remind herself of the things Ralph needed for his new regime. She was wandering round the shelves waiting for Jimbo to cut her two very lean lamb chops when Flick appeared with a friend.

'Hello, Lady Templeton.'

'Hello, Flick dear. I see you're managing very nicely without your sticks now. You must be pleased.'

'Yes, I am. The specialist says I've done extremely well, but he says it's only what he can expect from someone with as much guts as I've got.'

'Well, naturally.' Muriel smothered a smile. 'Who's this friend of yours?'

'This is Sebastian Prior from Prior's Farm. You must remember him? He's in my class at school and we both play the recorder too, don't we Sebastian? And we both share the same birthday. Isn't that odd?'

'It is indeed. Of course I remember you, Sebastian. My word, you have grown. When I played the piano in school you were quite the smallest boy in class. I can hardly recognise you.'

'I know, he's had a growing spell since he had his tonsils

out, haven't you?'

Sebastian nodded. Muriel studied his face. So this was Arthur Prior's grandson. The same very fair hair, the same dark brown eyes. The nose wasn't quite right, but that might come with age. The germ of an idea which had come to Muriel just before Ralph's heart attack emerged again in her mind. This might be the trigger she needed.

'Are you spending the afternoon with Flick?'

'Yes, he is.'

'Ask Mummy if you and Sebastian could come to tea with me and Sir Ralph, would you, Flick? Would you like that, Sebastian?'

'Yes, he would, wouldn't you? I certainly would.' Sebastian nodded.

'Tell her I'll bring you both safely back.'

While Muriel waited for Flick to run home to ask her mother, she finished her shopping. She remembered she needed stamps for Ralph. Muriel felt a tug at her skirt. It was Flick and Sebastian back.

'Mummy says yes, it's all right.'

The two children helped her to carry her shopping home. She hadn't yet heard Sebastian speak; no doubt he would, given half a chance. The accident hadn't put a stop to Flick's chatter.

Muriel opened the front door and said, 'Ralph! Ralph! Where are you, dear?'

'Here.' His reply came from the study. She opened the door and said, 'I've brought two visitors for tea. One is Flick and the other is her friend from school, they share the same birthday, isn't that a coincidence? He's called Sebastian Prior. I thought you'd enjoy talking to them both. Flick is walking without her sticks now, isn't that wonderful? Come in, children.'

Sebastian stood quietly in the doorway looking at Ralph, who had stood up abruptly when Muriel had told him the name of Flick's friend. Flick rushed straight in. 'Hello, Sir Ralph, you're looking much better than you were. Come in, Sebastian, come on.'

'You talk to my husband while I get the kettle on. Do you both drink tea?'

Sebastian nodded. Flick said 'Yes, we both do.'

When Muriel took the tea tray into the sitting room Ralph had already seated the children in there. He and Sebastian were talking about horses.

'You ride, then?'

'Oh yes, Sir Ralph, every weekend and in the holidays. My daddy rides too, when he's got time.'

'And your grandfather?'

'No, he's never learned.'

'I see. Do you ride sometimes, Flick?'

'No, but it would be a good idea.'

'Do you have your own pony, Sebastian?'

'No, I share with my sisters.'

'How many sisters have you got?'

'He's got four, haven't you? All older than him.'

'You've got cousins who ride though, haven't you?'

'No. My Auntie and Uncle haven't got any boys and girls.'

'I see.'

Muriel placed a small table beside each of the children, gave them napkins which they spread on their knees, and then served tea. Sebastian watched her pouring from the silver teapot with the coat of arms.

'Your teapot has letters on it. What do they say?'

Ralph explained. Sebastian brooded over the reply and then said, 'I see. Are you royal?'

'No, not royal at all, but a very old family, we go back about five hundred years.'

'I see. Silver teapots are very posh, aren't they?' Flick kicked his ankle and said, 'Shush.'

Ralph, feeling a little embarrassed by this conversation, said, 'Well, yes, I suppose they are.'

Muriel diverted Sebastian's curiosity by handing him a plate of chocolate biscuits.

'Thank you, Lady Templeton.' For some reason, Sebastian saying that drove home to Muriel the task she had set herself. It really was sad that this little boy was, in his own way, as much a Templeton as anyone alive, and yet he had no rights to silver teapots, nor titles, nor anything else. She patted his head as he took two of the biscuits. Flick took one and nibbled delicately. She was obviously enjoying being a grown-up.

Ralph and Flick and Sebastian chattered away together until Muriel finally had to say it was time they went or Flick's mummy would be wondering where they'd got to.

Ralph said, 'I could take Sebastian home.'

Flick jumped at the chance. 'In your Mercedes?'

'Yes.'

'Could I come too? It's only polite to take my guest home isn't it?'

'Oh yes. Muriel ring Harriet, please, my dear, and ask her if it would be convenient.'

It was and he did. Muriel stayed at home to clear up and left Ralph to take them himself.

When he got back he went straight to his study and stayed there until his evening meal was ready. Their dessert was pears poached in honey and lemon juice. When Ralph finished eating his, he laid down his spoon and said, 'Those pears were delicious, Muriel. The lamb chops were grilled to an absolute turn, and now all I need is my coffee and I shall be ready for anything.'

She poured his coffee for him, laying her hand over the sugar bowl as he reached for it. 'No! Ralph, remember!'

'Are you guilty of trying to organise me?'

'Well, you know you have to watch your weight, I'm only doing my wifely duty.'

'You were quite right to stop me putting sugar in my coffee, but I wasn't thinking of the sugar.'

Muriel looked down at her cup as she stirred in the sugar and said nothing.

'Well?' Ralph bent his head and tried to catch Muriel's eye.

'Only with the best of intentions. He's a very nice little boy, I knew him at school, you see, but of course I didn't know the rest of his story till you told me.'

'He is a very charming boy, when he gets a chance to speak! Have you noticed Flick limps quite badly?'

'Yes, but not nearly as badly as she did, she's improving all the time. He's got your colouring, well, till your hair went white.'

'Brown eyes and fair hair, you mean.'

'Yes. It's very distinctive. It does come out strongly in each generation, doesn't it? It must be an enduring link, musn't it?'

'What do you have in mind?'

'I have nothing in mind, Ralph, nothing at all.'

'Muriel!'

'No, really, I haven't anything specific in mind, truly I haven't, but I do feel something should be done.'

'I see. Give him or them money, you mean?'

'Oh no, indeed no, they'd be much too proud to take money, that wouldn't be right, something more significant needs to be done.'

'I don't really see why.'

'If you had descendants things would be different, but you haven't. So they are a branch of the family, aren't they, in a way.'

'Illegitimate.'

'Oh yes, but they can't be blamed for that. But it must be true or Sebastian wouldn't have the Templeton colouring. They'd just have been dismissed, so your grandfather knew – oh yes, he knew.'

'Yes. It's true all right. I'll think about it.'

'Did you meet anyone when you took him back.?'

'Arthur's son. Sebastian's father.'

'So what's Arthur's son like?'

'Tall, very tall, not like a Templeton, but the same colouring. Nice chap. Have you laid your plans for New York?'

'Are we going still? I thought perhaps you wouldn't, not after . . .'

'But yes, we are. We both said we'd carry on as usual and we shall. You can do your Christmas shopping on Fifth Avenue, how about that?'

'I should be terrified of getting lost in New York, you will look after me, won't you?'

'Of course. They'll be starting work on Hipkin Gardens while we're away. I know that's a long way off, but how about before the weather gets too inclement we have a little ceremony? You put in the first spade. What do you think?'

Muriel clapped her hands and said, 'Oh, what a lovely idea! We'll have reception here for everyone afterwards. Drinks and things to nibble, shall we? Whom shall we invite?'

They made a list. 'Add Arthur Prior and his wife to the list. See if they'll come.'

'Should we?'

'They can say no, can't they, if they don't want to come?'

'Oh dear, after the fuss they all made do you think *anyone* will accept?'

'Of course they will, they all love a chance for a chat and food. We'll have champagne, and you can cut the first sod with a silver spade.'

'Oh Ralph! We're not building the British Library or a museum or something. I think a brand new stainless steel one would be sufficient!'

Chapter 22

'Muriel!'

'In the kitchen, Ralph.' She glanced up as he came in. 'You're going out, dear?'

'Yes, I'm off up to town for the day.'

'To town? Today?'

'Yes, just something I need to talk over with the solicitor.'

She looked at his face, but could detect nothing that would give her a clue to his intentions. 'You're not driving up and back in one day?'

'No, I thought I'd take the train. Leave the car at the station.'

'How about if I pack you a bag and you stay overnight? It does seem a long way to go, there and back in a day. It's already nine o'clock.'

Ralph stood undecided. Muriel watched him, puzzled by his secretiveness. He looked out of the window for a moment and then said, 'Yes, I will then. If you're quick I shall be able to catch the ten five.'

'I'll be quick.'

Instinctively, Muriel didn't inquire his intentions, and

didn't ask to go with him. He'd been struggling with some dilemma ever since she'd brought little Sebastian home. Presumably he had come to some conclusions on which he needed legal advice. She waved him off, and then set about tidying up before going to the rectory for morning coffee. While she tidied up she worried. What right had she to interfere? The Priors were Ralph's problem not hers, but somehow the situation did need clarifying. She went to Caroline's very preoccupied.

Ralph came back in time for lunch the following day.

'You must have left very early, dear?'

'Caught the nine ten. It's a rattling good train, that one.'

'I'm making sandwiches because I hadn't expected you back so soon.'

'That's fine.'

Though the central heating was perfectly adequate, Muriel had lit the fire in their dining room because the weather had turned really cold. After lunch they pulled their chairs close to the fire while they drank their coffee.

'I know it's lunchtime, but I think I'll have a brandy. Just one.'

He pulled a side table towards his chair and placed his coffee and his brandy on it. Muriel waited. Before long he would tell her what he'd been doing in London.

'I've been up to see my solicitor.'

'Yes, I know.'

'Yes, well I listened to what you had to say and I've made a decision. You're quite right, something needs doing, and I've come up with the answer.'

'I see.'

'It's perfectly in order for me to go ahead, so I am.'

'I see.'

'In a way it's going against an old steadfast arrangement,

but I've got to do it.'

'I see.'

'When we shared everything when we married there was one thing we couldn't share, and that was Prior's Farm. That was under a completely separate arrangement and had to be kept in direct line because of its peculiar nature. So although I can ask you what you think, ultimately the decision is mine.'

'Ralph, I can't keep saying "I see" for much longer, because I don't see. What are you trying to tell me?'

'I've decided to . . . No, no, I was going to tell you the whole story, but frankly, Muriel, I think it would be a good idea if I didn't say anything until I get back home. You see, Arthur may not agree, and then I shall have to disappoint you by telling you it hasn't come off. Can you be patient with me a little longer?' Ralph smiled at her.

'Of course I can. I did want you to do something about straightening it out, but I didn't know what to suggest.'

'Well, what I've done I've done, let's hope he agrees. The solicitors were all for putting my ideas on to a pile of work needing attention. But I said no, I want it doing right now, not in ten years' time. This is a now decision, get your finger out and get it typed up, so I can come away with it in the morning. So they delivered it by messenger to the hotel this morning, about eight o'clock.'

'Are you going now?'

'No, it's market day, Arthur won't be back just yet.'

'How do you know?'

'Sebastian told me, he goes every week. So I'm going to lie down for a while and then set off and be back for dinner.'

'Very well, dear. Whatever it is you've done, I'm sure it will be right.'

'Let's hope so, this feud has got to be stopped. These old

wounds fester for generations, and there won't be another generation after me so I've got to be the one to make the move.'

'I do hope he doesn't take umbrage and refuse to accept. He has got a wild temper, as we've seen.'

'I'll do my best.'

Ralph had changed from his city suit into his tweeds before he left. He felt more comfortable wearing them, and they seemed more appropriate to the moment. The lane was just as smart and the yard, now sporting tubs of winter flowering pansies, still as neat as before.

There was no one around, so Ralph rang the door bell. He heard heavy footsteps crossing the yard, and turned to see who was coming. It was Arthur.

Ralph changed his briefcase over to his left hand and held his right hand out to Arthur. 'Good afternoon, Arthur. Had a good day at the market?'

Arthur shook his hand. 'How did you know?'

'Your Sebastian told me you usually went.'

'Good opportunity for meeting other farmers and seeing if they're doing as badly as yourself. What have you come to see me about?'

'It might take some time. Shall we sit on the wall?'

'If you like, or we can go inside.'

'Somewhere where we won't be overheard?'

'No, the children are home from school, so the house is full. Come in the stable.' He led the way across the yard to the end stable, opened the door, and invited Ralph inside. On top of some bales of hay he found two strong wooden crates, which he turned upside-down and placed on the stone floor. He invited Ralph to 'take a pew.'

'I'm very sorry about that time when I wouldn't pass the collection plate to you. The rector told me off and not half.

He's only a young man, but my word, he's got some kind of power, he has, he kind of sees right through you, and you've got to do what's right. I finished up apologising to him but I was too stubborn and angry at the time to apologise to you, but I am doing now.'

'That's all right, Arthur, your motives were honourable and that's what counts.'

'You're looking well now, bit thinner, but well. I come in here when I need to get away from them all, so I keep a bottle for private consumption, do you fancy a drop? Bryn's best, it is.'

'When I've finished what I've come to tell you, then yes, I'll be delighted.'

Ralph opened his briefcase and took out some papers. 'A lot of water's gone under the bridge since 1900. More than ninety years, and it's time things were put to rights. I've come to suggest . . . '

Arthur's face lit up. 'You don't mean you're going to suggest I buy the farm? Is that what you're going to say?'

'Well, not buy it exactly . . . '

'What then, what's your alternative? I've got the money all put by, just waiting for the day.'

'It is in my power to release you from this ridiculous peppercorn rent you pay, and I'm here to say there's no need to pay it any more.'

'Bloody hell, Ralph, I'm not poor. Twenty-five pounds a year isn't going to mean the difference between surviving or going under. What the hell!'

'Arthur!'

'Arthur nothing! If that's all you've come to tell me you can put yer papers away and skit. Whilst I pay that rent it's all legal; if I stop paying, then I'm under an obligation to you and I won't have it, absolutely not. I will *not* be under an obligation to *anyone* with the name of Templeton. My father was bitter to the end of his days about the way your family treated his mother and him. It wasn't his fault and it wasn't her fault, it was your grandfather's fault, but he never spoke to my father from the day he was born. Never acknowledged him, not once. He could pass him in the road and wouldn't even look at him. His own father! I'd have thought you'd have had more sense than to come here with a daft notion like you have. Go on, get off my land.' He sprang up from his crate and opened the bottom half of the stable door so Ralph could go. The horse in the stall whinnied its approval.

'You're too impulsive, Arthur. Be quiet and listen, we're getting too old for stupid misunderstandings, there've been enough of those in the past. You and I, between us, are putting a stop to the trouble. Sit down, and listen.'

'All right, then, all right.' He answered impatiently and still with half a mind to make Ralph leave, then on second thoughts he sat back down again and waited.

'Here are the deeds of the farm. Wallop Down Farm is its real name, did you know?'

'No! Wallop Down Farm? That's a daft name.'

'These deeds are yours and your children's. The farm is no longer owned by me nor any of my descendants. From today the farm is entirely yours and your children's, forever.'

The only sound in the stable was that of the horse gnawing the edge of the door. It stamped its feet and then whinnied joyously and then kicked the door. Ralph waited, observing the emotions flitting across Arthur's face; first anger, then delight, then anger again, then a strange kind of yearning. Arthur held the deeds in his hands, turning them over and over, relishing the feel of the strong thick parchment, and the sound of its crackling in his hands. His finger traced the lines of writing on the front as he looked across the yard to his house, and then back to the papers.

'I love this place. Love it, like I love nothing else. I love my boys and the grandchildren, but this,' – he thumped the door of the stall with his fist – 'this is me, it's in my bones. Each morning I open my eyes glad, no, *rejoicing* that I have fields in which I can walk, woods that are mine to tend, crops that are mine to harvest, animals that are mine to feed and care for. But there's always been that knowledge deep down that I was living a lie, because it wasn't really, truly, actually, mine. My pride tells me I should throw these' – he held up the deeds – 'back in your face and tell you I shan't accept favours from a Templeton, living or dead. But it's no good, I can't do that. If I die tomorrow I shall die a happy man now, and we can't ask more than that, can we?'

Ralph smiled and agreed. 'And now where's that drink we were going to have?'

Arthur stood up and, going behind the bales of hay, he brought out a bottle of Bryn's home-brewed ale and two glasses. He blew bits of hay out of the glasses and then poured them each a brimming glass.

The two men stood facing each other. Ralph proposed a toast. 'To Wallop Down Farm and the Priors!'

'To the Priors, and long may they reign at Wallop Down Farm!'

As Ralph was leaving, Arthur said, 'I've half a mind to change the name, do you know that? Daft name, but it has a ring to it and if that's its real name, why not?'

'Why not indeed?'

Chapter 23

Ralph propped up the spade in the hall and called for Muriel. 'I've collected the spade, dear, come and have a practice. The inscription looks good.'

Muriel came from the kitchen, wiping her hands on her apron. 'Oh Ralph, doesn't it look lovely! I shall feel like the Queen.' Muriel held the handle with both hands and rested her foot on the spade. 'I declare . . . ' She laughed and put the spade back against the wall. 'It's so shiny and new, and I love the words you've chosen. Hipkin Gardens, it does sound grand. My father would have been delighted if he knew.'

'Maybe the dead do know what the living are doing, so perhaps he does know.'

'Yes, maybe you're right. I'm well on with the nibbles and organising the table and the cutlery and things. I just need you to attend to the drinks side and I'm nearly ready. What's it like out?'

'Mild for the time of year, but most important, it's fine.'

'I do hope I don't let you down.'

'Of course you won't. You'll be just right. Memorised your speech?'

'For the twentieth time, yes. It's not long.'

'Doesn't need to be. I'm going for a rest after I've done the drinks. I'll lie on the bed and watch you getting ready.'

'That won't take long, I'm all clean on underneath. I've only got to take my dress off and put my new suit on. I've been thinking of buying trousers to wear on cold days in the winter. Would I look silly, do you think?'

'With your figure, Muriel, you'll look enchanting.'

'Thank you. You're so good for my self-esteem. I'd none before we married.'

'I've done you a good turn then?'

'Oh yes, indeed you have. I'm so pleased about Arthur and the farm. You did the right thing there.'

'It was your idea.'

'No it wasn't, it was yours.'

'You may not have suggested it, but you planted the seed.'

'Ralph, we must stop talking, I'm going to be late!'

'Muriel, you've never been late in your life!'

The sun came out as the crowd gathered to watch Muriel put in the first spade. Ralph had persuaded the builders to hang bunting around the trees, and they had improvised a small dais covered with a huge union jack for Muriel to stand on while she made her speech. There was quite a strong wind blowing and she was glad of the microphone; it was hateful to go to listen to a speech and then not be able to hear, and her voice wasn't strong. She felt incredibly nervous. There were far more people there than she had anticipated. Everyone had come round to Ralph's way of thinking and she was so grateful, if there'd been protesters there she would have been devastated. As it was she was having to summon up all her courage. Being on the sidelines fitted her personality better. She pulled the microphone down to her height and began her speech.

'Ladies and gentlemen. It gives me great pleasure on this wonderfully special day to plunge in the ceremonial spade, beautifully inscribed to commemorate this special occasion to which Ralph and I have looked forward for so long. As many of you will know, my father, and generations of my family before him, were head gardeners at the Big House. When the estate was sold we moved away and at the time I had no idea that I would ever come back here again. But life has come full circle and I'm standing here with Ralph my husband, whom I have to confess was a childhood sweetheart of mine' – the crowd cheered goodnaturedly at this – 'to inaugurate the start of the building of houses for the village. The two of us have planned and schemed and worried about the designs, because we so wanted the houses to be exactly right for country people to live in. A glazed porch over the back door for boots and the dog's water bowl, central heating, good-sized bedrooms, not rabbit hutches, two bathrooms so there's no queue in the mornings, and a good-sized garage because country people need cars nowadays, and if you haven't got one then you can always put the things you're saving for the scout jumble sale in there, and lovely pleasant gardens too. We shall be retaining most of the lovely trees which we all find so delightful, so Hipkin Gardens will be a lovely leafy place to live. We've already got three names on our list of people interested in renting, so hopefully they will all be occupied as they become ready. I do hope they will be a useful and pleasant addition to our village. I hereby declare the commencement of the building of Hipkin Gardens.'

Muriel stepped down from the dais and took hold of the spade. She grasped it tightly and, placing her foot on the top, pushed it firmly into the ground and removed the first sod.

Cheering and clapping broke out amongst the crowd and Muriel, having had her moment in the limelight, quietly stood back for Ralph to say a few words. He mentioned the opposition, but in a kindly and understanding way, and said how pleased he was that now everyone agreed that the eight houses would be of great benefit to the village. He caught Arthur's eye and smiled. A few of the crowd craned their necks to see who he was smiling at, and glanced at each other with knowing looks.

Finally, Peter said a prayer for the happiness and well-being of the people who would be living in the houses, and then Ralph asked everyone home for champagne.

Muriel and he led the way across the green to their house. She still missed Pericles running to greet her when she came home, but the press of all their friends and neighbours pouring up the lane behind them put him out of her mind.

For the first half an hour Muriel was frantically busy attending to everyone's needs. Ralph and Peter opened the champagne and Ralph proposed a toast 'To Hipkin Gardens!' They all clinked their glasses and drank the toast and then flocked to the dining room, where Muriel had laid out the food. There were people everywhere, in the sitting room, squeezed in the study, sitting on the stairs, and the hubbub was deafening.

Deep in conversation on the stairs were Venetia Mayer and Pat. Ralph offered to refill their glasses. 'Oh, yes please, Sir Ralph. Thank you very much.' Pat took a sip of her champagne and listened to Venetia chatting up her host.

'Thank you, Sir Ralph. What a lovely speech Lady Templeton gave. You've done the village a really good turn deciding to build these houses. It's just what's needed. Glad to see you looking so much better, you gave us all quite a turn when you had your heart attack, it's lovely to see you up and about. And looking so well. It certainly hasn't harmed your good looks. Still as handsome as ever!'

Ralph bowed in acknowledgement. Pat nudged Venetia. 'I don't know how you dare to speak to him like that.'

'Like what? I was only making him feel good. I read somewhere that you should try to make everyone you meet feel better for having spoken to you, so that's what I was doing.'

'Oh yes, sometimes you do go over the top with it though. Especially with one person I could mention.'

'Who's that?'

'Craddock Fitch.'

At the mention of his name Venetia jumped and knocked Pat's elbow, whereupon she spilled her champagne and it splashed on Venetia's suit.

'Oh, I'm so sorry, it hasn't spoiled it, has it?'

'No, I'll dab it off, it'll be all right.'

Pat watched her drying the splashes and, not to be put off by the incident, pressed home with her quest for some inside information.

'He seems to come to the Big House a lot.'

'Well, he's interested in making sure everyone is satisfied.'

'Is *he* satisfied?' Pat said with a knowing wink.

Venetia wriggled out of that by saying, 'Jeremy would be sacked and so would I if he wasn't satisfied with our work.'

Venetia grinned. Pat gave her a dig in the ribs and a wink. 'Yer can't do nothing in this village yer know, without us all finding out. I've written to Mr Fitch. Done it all official like. Told 'im we want to move into the house and Dad get the job permanent. Oh Venetia, yer've no idea how much

I'm looking forward to it. A big house, all those bedrooms, and with our Dean studying so much it's just what he needs, his own room.'

'I'm quite envious of you Pat. It's a lovely house. That view across Sykes Wood!'

'I know. I've looked round it with the kids and mi dad. Our Michelle's in 'er element. She's in charge of the gardening at the school, yer know. Green fingers, Mr Palmer says she has. So she's looking forward to 'elping Dad. And really it's you I've got to thank for putting in a good word for us.'

'That's all right, Pat. You can invite me to tea one day when you get settled.'

'Oh, right I will. Can't invite yer where I live now, but when we've moved I will, that's a date. Just going to find the bathroom.'

'With the new house, and working for Jimbo and the school, things are looking up for you, aren't they?'

Pat gave Venetia a thumbs-up and wandered off. She requested directions and Muriel pointed her the way. As she went up the stairs she heard voices. Rounding the bend she came upon Linda from the Store and Alan Crimble. They were standing close together on the landing. Alan was holding Linda's hand and she was straightening his hair. 'You should comb it over to this side, Alan, it looks more modern like that. Oh!' They hastily broke apart when they saw Pat.

'What are you two up to then? Canoodling, eh? Whatever next?'

Linda retorted, 'You mind your own business, Pat Duckett.'

Alan patted Linda's arm. 'Now, now, Linda.' He spoke to Pat. 'Linda and me's going out together.'

'Oh, my word. That's a turn-up for the book. What a surprise!'

Rather defiantly, Linda began to say, 'We've been going out since . . . '

'Since that day I saved Sir Ralph's life. That's when it started.'

'I thought how wonderful he was. Saving a life like that.' She gazed up at him adoringly.

'Well, he was wonderful. Certainly redeemed himself, and no mistake.'

'In fact, you can be the first to know.' Alan took hold of Linda's hand. 'We're getting engaged at Christmas.'

'Engaged! That's quick work, I must say. Still neither of yer's spring chickens. You must be thirty-seven or eight, Linda, if yer a day. Yer've worked in the Store since before I got married. You've seen some changes there, and not half. Remember old Mrs Thornton? Disgusting it was. No hygiene at all. And you, Alan, 'ow old are you?'

'Thirty-two.'

'Well then, there you are. Why waste time 'anging about. Get on with it, I say. Have yer planned where yer going to live?'

'We're thinking of asking to rent one of Sir Ralph's houses.'

'Good idea. Considering what you did for 'im, yer should be top of the list. Got to go, I'm dying.'

As Pat returned downstairs into the fray she found the rectory twins sitting side by side on the bottom step. Alex had a piece of cake in his hand, and Beth a small bowl filled with crisps. She was feeding them to Alex, who was obediently eating them. In between she kept popping one into her own mouth.

'Well now, you two, can your Auntie Pat squeeze

between you?' They both looked up. Beth shuffled along a little and made enough room for Pat to get by. She paused for a moment and watched them. Beth was dressed in a dark-pink flowered long-sleeved dress, with a white collar and cuffs. In her blonde curly hair Caroline had tied a matching ribbon. Her tights were dark-pink, and on her feet she had a pair of black patent leather shoes. Alex was dressed in red; red tartan shirt with a bow tie, matching tartan trousers and a smart plain red waistcoat. For once, his mop of reddish-blond hair was neatly combed and smoothed down. They both looked up at her and smiled.

Beth offered her a crisp. 'Cri'p, Aun'ie Pa'?'

'Oh, thank you, Beth. Talking, are yer now?'

Alex shouted. 'Yes!'

Caroline came rushing out of the dining room. 'Oh! Thank goodness they're there. I need eyes at the back of my head with these two. They're into everything.'

'Aren't they growing up? Beth's just given me a crisp. She called me Auntie Pat.'

'Really? She's just begun talking, actually. Peter's been quite worried about her. She's always let Alex do it all up until now. So pleased to hear about the house, Pat. You must be delighted. I haven't met your father, is he here?'

'No. Doesn't socialise much. And he's a teetotaller, so you won't be seeing him in The Royal Oak either. Soon as the paperwork's gone through we'll be moving in. Can't wait.'

'You deserve it, Pat.'

'Can I ask something? Will you and the rector be going to the Bonfire Party up at the Big House?'

'We've had an invite popped through the door, and I think probably we shall. It is awkward though, isn't it?' She nodded her head in the direction of Ralph, who was seeing someone off at the door.

'Exactly. I mean, I can't refuse in the circumstances. Do you know if Sir Ralph's going?'

'No idea. Haven't mentioned it. Bit tricky really.' Caroline smiled at her, scooped up the twins, one under each arm, because they'd begun to sprinkle crisps on Muriel's hall carpet, and went to find Peter. It was time they went; the twins had behaved well for quite long enough, and she could see problems arising shortly.

'Excuse me, darling, I think it's time we went home.' The twins began protesting, wriggling and shouting to get down. Peter took Beth from under Caroline's right arm and swung her up into the air. Alex shouted, 'Alex. Dada. Alex. Up.' He swung Beth up twice more and then put her down and picked up Alex. He swung him up into the air and Alex screamed his delight.

'Peter! We really must go!'

'Yes, we must. Before trouble starts. Right, Alex, that's enough. Off we go. Go find Auntie Moo and Uncle Ralph.' They found them by the front door saying goodbyes.

Sheila Bissett and Ron were just leaving. 'Thank you so much for inviting us, we have enjoyed ourselves, haven't we Ron? These houses can only be good for the village, I'm so pleased it's all going ahead. See you at the Bonfire Party!' She twinkled her fingers at Ralph and stepped out into the road. Ron shook hands with Muriel and Ralph and followed her across the green.

Caroline kissed Muriel and thanked her. 'Do hope the twins haven't made too much mess. They're just at that age. Sorry.'

Ralph said, 'Don't worry, they've behaved excellently for two such small people.' He patted their heads, but Beth reached up and pursed her lips. She wanted to give him a kiss. So he bent down and she kissed him. 'Bye, bye, Raff. Bye, bye, Moo.' She leapt off the threshold and landed on the stone step. Peter caught her hand before she ran into the road. The four of them waved and went up Church Lane to the rectory.

Muriel and Ralph stayed by the door to say goodbye to all their guests.

'Thank you for coming.'

'Glad you enjoyed it.'

'Thanks for your help.'

'Thank you again, it's been lovely.'

'Mind how you drive after all that champagne!'

Arthur and his wife Celia were among the last to leave. Arthur shook Ralph's hand and said, 'Thanks, Ralph, for inviting us. I'm very pleased about the houses, it's a grand gesture which will revitalise the village.'

Ralph smiled. 'Thank you, I'm glad I've got your approval. Glad you've forgiven me! That grandson of yours, Sebastian, is a charming boy, you must be proud of him.'

Arthur acknowledged the compliment and said 'We're proud of the girls too, aren't we Celia?' They stepped out into the road and waved goodbye.

Harriet kissed Ralph and Muriel and said, 'Glad you got your own way, it's a very good thing for the village. I knew they'd all come round in the end.'

Jimbo said, 'Got to dash, children home from school soon. Thanks for a lovely time. Come along, Harriet. We shall be late.'

Muriel fell into bed that night completely exhausted. She listened for Ralph bringing up her camomile tea. She needed something to calm her jangled nerves. Still, the whole event had been a complete success. She'd provided far too much food, but most of it she'd put in the freezer for another time. So many people had come to the ceremony. Thank goodness they'd all decided to approve. She couldn't bear disharmony, no, she really couldn't.

She could hear Ralph coming up the stairs. He laid the tray on her bedside table. 'Thank you for making it such a splendid day, Muriel. You were wonderful. Can a husband give his very best and only wife a thank-you gift?'

'Oh Ralph!' Muriel sat up. 'Have you bought me a present?' He sat on the edge of the bed.

'Yes, I have. It took a lot of choosing. I do hope you like it. I do know it's the right size.' From his dressing-gown pocket he took a small velvet box. Muriel almost snatched it from him. She'd never grown blasé about his gifts; she was still as she had been as a child, so grateful that someone thought enough about her to buy her a present.

She lifted the lid of the tiny box and inside, nestled in the black velvet, was the most beautiful diamond ring she had ever seen. It had a big central diamond and on either side a triangle of smaller diamonds. The stones glinted and sparkled in the light from her lamp.

'Oh Ralph, I love my engagement ring but this . . . why, it's wonderful. Just wonderful.' He put it on her finger and it fitted perfectly.

She kissed him and said, 'Thank you, dear, from the bottom of my heart. I'm so happy. I've got you, and everyone in the village likes what we're doing about the spare land, so everything in the garden is lovely. I couldn't be any happier. No, I really couldn't.'

Chapter 24

But there was just one matter which was worrying Muriel, and she hadn't yet found the right words to introduce it to Ralph. Considering the blinding mistake she'd made when the problem first arose, it was more than likely she never would find the right words.

She decided to ask Jimbo's advice. No, she'd ask Caroline's advice; Jimbo was too involved. Yes, she'd ask Caroline for coffee, no she wouldn't, because she couldn't guarantee Ralph wouldn't be in. No, she'd go to the rectory or perhaps catch Caroline in the Store or helping at the church with something. Yes, she'd ask her then. Because it was already 1 November and only four more days to go. He'd read the leaflet with his morning post, he must have seen the posters in the church hall and in the church porch, and yet he'd never said a word.

No, she wouldn't wait, she'd go round this morning. Caroline never minded visitors, though sometimes it was possible to catch her at the most inopportune moments. Alex and Beth had certainly changed the lifestyle in the rectory. She remembered the day she had called round with some things for the white elephant stall, and there was water dripping through the kitchen ceiling because Alex had managed to turn the washbasin tap full on and it had overflowed, Beth had scribbled on some work Peter had ready to go to the printers, and Caroline had just found that Alex had come down the stairs with a crayon in his hand and drawn a line on the wallpaper all the way down.

Muriel called about eleven. Sylvia had taken the twins out for a walk in their pushchair, in the rather vain hope that they would both fall asleep for a while. Caroline was clearing up toys, and Peter was in his study.

'Is it Peter you've come to see?'

'No, it's you. Is it convenient?'

'It is. I'm just about to stop for coffee. Then when Sylvia comes back I shall take over and she can have hers. Come through into the kitchen.'

They chatted about this and that, and when the coffee was ready Caroline sat in her rocking chair and said, 'I'm all ears.' Muriel sat at the kitchen table because rocking chairs made her feel seasick.

'The Bonfire Party.'

'Oh yes. Are you going?'

'Well, that's just it. Normally Ralph and I discuss everything, but I made such a mess of it at the dinner party I daren't mention it, and he hasn't either. Are you going?'

'Apparently most of the village is waiting to hear what Ralph is doing.'

'Oh dear. I desperately want to go. I know it won't be the same as when I was a child, but it was the highlight of the year for me. The smell of the woodsmoke, the cold wind up on the field, the feel of the hot potato through my gloves, and the frizzling of the sparklers. I loved it all.'

'Well, Peter and I . . . ' The doorbell rang. 'Excuse me,

I'll go and answer that. Peter's writing his sermon, he won't want disturbing.'

Muriel could hear voices in the hall, and then Peter's study door opening. Caroline came back into the kitchen and said, 'That was Craddock Fitch for Peter. Peter and I are going. With it starting at six, we're taking the twins for an hour and then coming home.'

'I see.'

'Me being me, I think being honest is best. Quite simply, ask him if he's going. Straight out. If he definitely doesn't want to go, but if you decide you do, come in the car with us. We can squeeze you in, the only problem is I think the fireworks will frighten the children, they're a bit young for revelling in loud bangs, so we may come home early. It will be good fun, won't it? It will be quite like old times, really, for you.'

'I won't go if he won't, thank you all the same. No, I couldn't.' She gazed out of the kitchen window, deep in thought. She was being childish. She wouldn't mention it. She hadn't got Caroline's sound common sense. No, she'd leave it to Ralph.

They heard the study door open: Peter's voice boomed out across the hall. 'Caroline! have you a minute?'

'Excuse me, I won't be long.'

Muriel heard a shriek of delight from Caroline, a lot of laughter, and her saying, 'Unbelievable. Many, many thanks. Greatly appreciated. The village will be delighted. We can go straight ahead now. That's solved all our problems, believe me.'

What on earth were they talking about? The front door shut and Peter and Caroline came into the kitchen. Peter was waving a piece of paper in the air.

'Muriel! Believe it or believe it not, Craddock Fitch has

just given us fifteen thousand pounds for the church central heating! Can you imagine that? Look, here it is.' He held the cheque for Muriel to see. In bold, confident writing were the words 'fifteen thousand pounds' and a flourishing signature; H. Craddock Fitch.

In a tone somewhat less than enthusiastic, Muriel said, 'How wonderful.' This cheque made matters even worse. Fifteen thousand pounds to buy himself the position of Lord of the Manor. That was Ralph's place. Yes, it was. He was the gentleman. Close to tears, she stood up, thanked Caroline for the coffee and her advice, and went home.

Peter and Caroline looked at each other.

Peter asked. 'Should I go after her?'

'No, leave it. She and Ralph need to get things straight between them. This cheque blessed well won't have helped, though. You can see his strategy, can't you? Paying for the heating, reintroducing the Bonfire Party, buying Pat's cottage. It's as plain as the nose on your face. An awful lot will depend on whether Ralph decides to go to the Party on Saturday.'

Muriel found she'd locked herself out, so she had to ring the bell.

'I'm so sorry, I forgot my key.'

'You're back early. I thought you would be gone for the morning. Caroline busy, is she?'

'Sylvia had the twins out in the pushchair, and Peter was writing his sermon, so we had the kitchen to ourselves.'

'You didn't stay long, though?'

'No, I didn't. Oh, you've had coffee.'

'Yes, I am capable of making my own you know, my dear. Well, sometimes.'

'I see. I'll just go and do some little jobs upstairs. I've the ironing to put away, and I want to get your suit out ready for the cleaners and . . . '

Ralph took her hand. 'Muriel, my dear. What is the matter? I can see you're upset. Tell me, please, and if I can put it right I shall. Nil desperandum.'

'I don't want to hurt *anyone* and most of all I don't want to hurt you. But I have done, or rather I *did* do. Now I can't mention it again.' Muriel paused for a moment and then continued. 'But I've got to.'

'Come in the sitting room and sit beside me and tell me everything. What are husbands for if not for solving problems?'

'But that's just it. You *are* the problem.'

'Me?' He struck an attitude of mock despair. 'Are you – are you wanting a divorce? So soon! So soon!'

'Ralph! How could you? I'm going to come straight out with it.' She took a deep breath and asked, 'Are we going to the party on Saturday up at the Big House?'

He let go of her hand. 'Ah!'

'Apparently the village is waiting to see what you are going to do.'

'Are they indeed?'

'Matters are even worse than that. You know he's buying Pat's cottage, and who can blame her? Well, now, this morning, he's been to the rectory and given Peter the fifteen thousand pounds to pay for the church heating. Something we couldn't expect he could refuse, either. So now you know it all. And I'm sorry and I don't know what to do. And oh! Ralph I *do* want to go to the party, but if you say no then no it will be.'

Ralph stood up and went to the window looking out over the green.

'Has he, by Jove? Determined devil, isn't he? Just think. When my father went to war in 1939 he owned every cottage in this village. His ancestors gave the church the land it stands on, he owned the woods, the fields, the spare land, Prior's Farm, and his word was law round here. In the space of just fifty years all I own is this house, which I've had to buy, and now the spare land and by the middle of next year eight houses on it. Times change.' He stood lost in thought. Muriel sat watching, twisting her handkerchief round and round in her hands. Twice she nearly spoke, and twice she resisted the temptation.

When he did continue, his tone was so vehement he made her jump. 'I'm damned if that chap is going to get the better of me. Financially he very definitely has the edge, but where the people of this village are concerned, if I can keep faith with them, he won't win in the end. He might think he has, but he won't have. So yes, damn it, we shall go, and we shall damned well enjoy ourselves, or at least look as if we are. Make sure everyone knows.'

Muriel clapped her hands and rushed across the room to him. She took his hands in hers and kissed them both. 'Oh Ralph, what a good decision. How absolutely perfectly right. Don't worry, I'll make sure they all know. That Oriana Duncan-Lewis will spoil it for me, her lighting the bonfire, indeed! But I shall look the other way till she's done it.'

Ralph smiled indulgently. 'It won't alter anything, doing that.'

'No, it won't, but it will make *me* feel better! I really think I might need some extra bits and pieces for lunch. I'm off to the Store.' She set off with a glad heart; in fact she felt like standing in the middle of the green and shouting out her news to whoever cared to listen. She just hoped the Store would be full of people and then the news would spread like wildfire.

Sadie Beauchamp was at the till when she went in, and best of all there were plenty of customers about.

Sadie called out, 'Morning, Muriel. How's things?'

'Oh very good, thank you, Sadie. Yes, very good indeed.' In a loud voice she asked, 'Shall we be seeing you at the bonfire on Saturday?'

Barry's mother's head popped up over the top of the breakfast cereals. 'You going then, Lady Templeton?'

'Oh yes, indeed we are. My husband and I are really looking forward to it. Let's hope the weather's good.'

'Oh, well, that's all right then, we didn't want to miss all the fun.' She raised her voice and shouted, ''Ear that, everybody? Sir Ralph's going! I hear there's going to be a big buffet in the marquee! They've been putting it up this week.'

'Really?'

'Oh yes, Mr Charter-Plackett's catering so it's bound to be good.'

'And there's going to be toffee apples and presents for any children going.'

'And Mr Charter-Plackett's doing the fireworks, isn't he, Mrs Beauchamp?'

'Yes, he's up there now planning it all.'

'Hope he's got some o' them mighty big rockets. I love seeing them going up.'

'There's to be a Guy Fawkes. Specially made with fireworks in 'im.'

'No! Just 'ope it doesn't look like old Fitch! Not after the last time. Right put the lid on it, that would!'

'Who's lighting the bonfire, Mrs Beauchamp?'

'As I do not have the ear of Mr Fitch, I'm afraid I can't help you on that score.'

Barry's mother nudged her neighbour. 'Liar. We all know she knew him years ago, and they've been seen out together. Sat in the back of his Roller with the chauffeur strutting his stuff in the front.'

'No! Really?'

Barry's mother nudged her neighbour again and whispered, 'Bit of blooming good luck for her and not half, he's a right catch, with all that money. Bit of a cold fish, but so what? Wouldn't mind him myself.'

'Get on, what would your Vince say?'

'I wouldn't ask him!' They chortled together behind the cereals, but Muriel ignored them. If Barry's mother knew, then the whole village would know before long. Satisfied with her efforts she paid for her shopping and left. As she stepped out into Stocks Row, she found Sheila Bissett tying Pom to the post Jimbo had provided for dog owners.

'Good morning, Sheila.'

'Good morning, Muriel. I do miss seeing your Pericles out and about. I expect you miss him too.'

'Oh yes, I do. Good morning, Pom.' She bent down to stroke him. 'He does do well for his age, doesn't he?'

'Shall we be seeing you on Saturday? You and Sir Ralph?'

'Yes, you shall. We're really looking forward to it.'

'Oh good. It'll be a bit upsetting for you both, but time marches on, doesn't it? We all have to adapt.'

'Yes, we do. Let's hope it doesn't rain.'

'Let's hope so.'

Chapter 25

In the dark of the early evening of Guy Fawkes Day, Pat Duckett, Dean and Michelle were standing outside the Head Gardener's house, savouring thoughts about moving in.

'Won't it be lovely, Mum? A whole big bedroom to myself. And one for you too.' Michelle gazed up at the blank windows, picturing herself sitting at one of them looking out over the gardens, wearing a beautiful white dress with an open book resting on her lap, like that lady she'd seen in that old film on the telly.

Dean kicked a lump of brick across the rough grass. 'I'll need a desk, Mum. With a chair and some bookshelves. I'll have to have a bike. Can't walk all that way to the school bus and back.'

'So will I, won't I Mum?'

Pat nodded. 'We'll all three need bikes. And you'll need a new bed, Dean. That one of yours is going to the tip. We'll get you a lovely long one. Yer growing that fast, you'll be needing a chair at the end for yer feet with that old thing you've got now. Wonder if yer Grandad still has his driving licence. Maybe we could even afford a car after a while.

Then 'e could take us out for rides. Might even go on 'oliday.'

Michelle's eyes lit up. 'On holiday? Oh Mum, just think, on holiday!'

'We'll have to watch the pennies, mind. No silly spending. Perhaps we could rent a cottage by the sea. Yes, I'd fancy . . . ' She heard footsteps in the dark. 'Who's there? Who is it?'

'Only me!' Through the gloom the three of them could see the outline of Grandad. He came to stand beside them. 'Come to see our new abode. By heck, kids, we've landed on our feet here, haven't we?' He gazed up at the front of the house. 'Chosen which bedroom you want? I'd like one big enough to have a comfortable chair in it with my own telly. Can't stand them daft programmes you kids watch.'

Michelle said her grandad could have the biggest one, then. 'Right thanks, that'll do nicely. Greenwood Stubbs, Head Gardener, accepts with pleasure. You and me, we'll turn this place round and not half, Michelle.' He gave her a friendly conspiratorial nudge. 'All it needs is dedication, and I've got plenty of that. Don't expect you'll be helping, will yer, Dean?'

'Might. If yer pay me.'

'Oh. Well, we'll need casual labour from time to time, so I'll put you at the top of my list.'

'Put Rhett on yer list as well, Grandad.'

'Rhett? Who's he when he's at home?'

'Rhett Wright from next door.'

'We'll put his name down as well then. With a moniker like that he needs all the help he can get. Will he work hard, though?'

'Do anything for money, will Rhett. Come on then.'

Pat asked, 'Shall we need net curtains, do you think?' But

no one answered, they'd all set off to the bonfire.

She stood listening to the silence. Be lovely living up here. What with the bathroom, and the modern kitchen. A whole new start. Well, wherever you are Duggie, either down there or up yonder, at least now yer know the Ducketts are doing better than expected. Oh yes, much better than expected. Yes, this Christmas was looking good. She'd be off to the sales after, buying furniture and things. She ambled off, hampered by her fur boots and thick trousers. Pat pushed her scarf back from her face and, looking up at the clear starry sky, watched a rocket exploding. That was just how she felt. Explosive. Yes, exploding with joy.

Pat cut through the neglected kitchen garden, opened the door in the wall and stepped out onto the path. From where she stood she could see the crowds arriving for the Party. Old Fitch had erected floodlights so the whole of Home Farm field was illuminated. The marquee erected to one side was glowing softly, and people were going in and out carrying trays and boxes. The bonfire was enormous. You could have thought it was Coronation night or something. Perched right on top was the guy. She chuckled to herself. What a scream it had been, making that dummy of old Fitch. It was Dean's idea to spray a mophead for his hair. Looked a treat, it did. What a laugh they'd had, but it'd done the trick. If ever he found out she'd helped . . . Ruthless, he was. But no matter, he'd transformed her life. She went gleefully down the slope to join the throng.

Muriel and Ralph were walking to Home Farm field by cutting through the churchyard and using the little gate in the wall, which had been put there dozens of years ago so that the Templetons could walk to church from the Big House without having to go the roundabout way via the drive. The gate was stiff, and Ralph had to struggle with it to get it open. Weeds had twined themselves around it and grass was growing in the hinges.

Muriel held the torch for him while he forced it open. 'We shouldn't really be using this, should we?'

'He won't know, will he? I don't expect anyone else remembers about this gate.'

'I do. It's a special gate for me. You stand that side and I'll stand this side and we'll kiss like we did when we thought we were leaving Turnham Malpas forever. I was twelve and you were fourteen. I can even remember the dress I was wearing.' They had their commemorative kiss, and then hand in hand in the dark they wended their way along the disused path towards the floodlit field. 'I'm determined to enjoy myself tonight, no matter what.'

Ralph squeezed her hand. 'So am I. I hear there's a beer tent as well as the marquee, so I shall visit that and get my money's worth out of him!'

'Well, as you're not driving, I expect you can. Do you know, I've never seen you worse for drink?'

'My dear, you never shall. Merry, perhaps, but never under the influence. Have you a key in case we lose each other?'

Muriel felt in her coat pocket. 'Yes, I have.' Her eyes alight with anticipation, she strode forward. Ralph looked at her face as they came within the arc of the floodlights. She looked not a day older than twelve. No one looking at her now could imagine for one moment the heights of passion he had released in her. He just hoped they had plenty more years left in which to enjoy their new-found delights, despite this dratted heart business. He felt a tug at his overcoat. Looking down he found little Beth standing beside him, her mouth pursed ready for a kiss. 'Raff! Ki'.

Raff.' He bent down to receive her kiss. 'Now, Beth, where's your Mummy? Muriel! just a moment dear, Beth's here and there's no one with her.'

'Oh dear. Oh dear. Caroline will be desperate. Beth, where's Mummy? Where is she?'

'Mummy gone.' She put her hand confidently in Muriel's. Ralph and Muriel anxiously scanned the growing crowd. Then Ralph shouted, 'That's Peter, over there. He looks frantic.' Ralph shouted and waved his arms and Peter, turning his head this way and that in his anxious search for Beth, suddenly caught sight of Ralph and came running across.

'Thank God!' He swung Beth up into his arms and hugged her. 'Daddy's been wondering where you were, Beth. I'm sorry, but you're going to have your reins on.' She began struggling when she saw him pull the reins out of his pocket. 'No. No.'

'Yes. Yes. Sorry.' He persevered with Beth as she twisted this way and that to stop him getting the reins on her. 'Caroline has Alex and I'm supposed to be in charge of Beth, I'm not doing a very good job, am I? There, young lady, that's you secure. Aren't we lucky having such a wonderful evening for the bonfire? It's all going to be perfectly splendid. I have never seen such a huge bonfire, have you?'

'No. But then he would want the biggest and the best!' Ralph commented. Peter looked sorrowfully at him and Ralph apologised. 'Sorry. He is trying hard, too hard perhaps. Come, Muriel, into the fray.'

Peter relayed a message to them. 'Mr Fitch has suggested we use the front hall for our drinks and buffet. He said if I saw you would I say you would be most welcome to join him, before the fire is lit. They're turning out the floodlights at a quarter past six and then lighting the bonfire. So you're invited right now.'

'Shall we go, my dear?'

'Oh yes, just to be polite, but then I want to be outside after that.'

'Of course. Lead the way, Peter.' Ralph found Beth's little hand stealing a grip on his, and she wanted Peter and him to swing her as they walked. Ralph had a lump in his throat.

The hall was brightly lit. The reception desk had been cleared of papers and telephones and a small buffet had been laid out. Behind the buffet stood Venetia, and by a small table beside the desk stood Jeremy, helping to serve drinks. Oriana, Sadie, and Mr Fitch were already there, and Caroline too, with Alex.

Venetia, looking tense, was serving Oriana with a plate of food. 'A couple of canapés too? So fattening all these things, aren't they, but so tempting. We've Jimbo to blame for that. He always caters so wonderfully you can't resist. Staying the night, are you?'

Oriana Duncan-Lewis pointedly ignored Venetia's question. 'That will be sufficient, thank you. I'll get myself a drink. Oh, there's champagne! Craddock knows how much I love champagne. He's such a dear, isn't he, and so thoughtful.'

Venetia, unsettled by Oriana's imperious manner and seething with jealousy, answered between gritted teeth. 'Very thoughtful, oh yes. Always so considerate.' Oriana's reply was a scathing look. She thanked Jeremy for the champagne he'd handed to her. Knowing that Venetia was watching, she caught Mr Fitch's eye and with a very possessive, intimate look silently toasted him.

He briskly acknowledged her salute and then went to

welcome Ralph and Muriel. Shaking hands with them, he said, 'Please call me Craddock. It's ridiculous to be excessively formal nowadays. May I call you Ralph and Muriel?' The two of them agreed. Taking Muriel to the buffet, he asked her what she would like. 'I'll have a gin and tonic but nothing to eat, thank you, Craddock. I will take a jacket potato to eat by the bonfire, if you don't mind.'

'Not at all. Do exactly as you wish. You're my guest, so help yourself whenever you wish. I'm delighted that you've come. I'm here to stay, so we may as well get on with each other as best we can. I shall be having the Village Show here too. Is it possible I might be able to enlist your help with that?' He smiled at her.

Muriel replied, 'I should have to give it my consideration.'

'Please do. We can't let the village miss out just because we don't see eye to eye, can we?' He looked at his watch. 'It's almost time for lighting the bonfire. Where's Oriana?' He looked across the hall at her. She didn't reply because she was having an angry confrontation with Sadie.

'I've told you, I mean what I say!'

Sadie laughed. 'So, we go, just once, to the theatre to a première for which Craddock had been given two tickets. That hardly constitutes a major relationship.'

'Well, don't you get any bright ideas. He's mine and don't you forget it.'

'Yours?' Sadie laughed. 'Since when has anyone been able to claim Henry Craddock Fitch as their own?'

'As from now. Keep off!'

The two of them became aware that their raised voices were being overheard. Oriana looked highly embarrassed. Sadie merely looked amused. 'Craddock, I understand Oriana has a ball and chain attached to your ankle.' She pointedly studied his feet. 'I can't see it?' Oriana flushed dark red.

Mr Fitch snapped out his answer. 'You won't. There isn't one. I think, my dear Oriana, you've overstepped the mark.'

'Overstepped the mark? But you and I . . .'

Mr Fitch grimaced '. . . Are friends, that's all. Sadie is a lady who holds a special place in my esteem. I don't care to have her spoken to in such a manner.'

Oriana became not only indignant but very angry. In a low voice she said, 'How dare you treat me in such a cavalier fashion in front of your guests? How dare you?'

Sadie intervened. 'Steady, Oriana, it never does to throw a temper with Craddock. I did once, and lived to regret it.'

'I shall throw as many tempers as I like. Well, Craddock, you haven't answered my question.' Glass in hand she went towards him. He stared fixedly at her and asked, 'I've forgotten. What was the question?'

For the moment anger had got the better of her and she couldn't remember. Mr Fitch laughed. 'Come, come, do calm down. Storm in a teacup.'

His patronising tone angered her even more and, frustrated at not being able to better him verbally, she threw the contents of her glass straight in his face. In a very controlled way he withdrew his handkerchief from his top pocket and wiped his face dry. When he had dried himself to his satisfaction he opened his mouth to speak, but Oriana forestalled him by screeching, 'You can light your own damned bonfire,' and storming out, leaving the assembled company stunned into silence. Before they had recovered themselves she returned to pick up her bag, which Alex had found and was taking to show his mother. She snatched it from his hands and as she stormed out a second time she shouted over her shoulder, 'I just wish you were the guy on top!'

Alex cried, Beth cried in sympathy, Muriel went bright red and Craddock Fitch stood grey-faced and tight-lipped. Ralph gave a wry smile, remembering just in time to turn his back to the other guests so they couldn't see how amused he was. Venetia, delighted at the turn of events, silently toasted Oriana with champagne. Sadie drained her glass and said 'Well! That brought that little confrontation to a satisfactory conclusion!' She picked up her gloves and left.

Muriel, in a rather high squeaking voice, said, 'I think I'll go outside to see what's going on.' Others followed her lead and they trailed after her, leaving Ralph and Mr Fitch alone.

'Well, Ralph, after that exhibition of ill breeding I appear to have no one to light my bonfire. Would you do me the honour? It would look foolish for me to light my own.'

'Yes, I will.'

'Thank you. Let's go.'

As they went out of the front door and crossed the lawn to the field, Arthur Prior and his family were crossing it on their way to join the party. 'Good evening, Arthur. Have you met Craddock Fitch?'

'No, we haven't had the pleasure.'

'May I introduce my cousin and his family, Craddock?' While he was doing the introductions an idea occured to Ralph. 'Now Sebastian, how would it be if you helped me to light the bonfire? Mr Fitch wouldn't mind, would you?'

'Of course not. He isn't a grandson of yours, is he? No, he can't be, of course he can't.'

'Unfortunately no, he isn't, but he's the next best thing.' Ralph took Sebastian's hand in his and together they marched with Mr Fitch onto the Home Farm field. At a signal from him the floodlights were turned out, someone played a fanfare on a trumpet, and Ralph and Sebastian stepped forward to ignite the biggest bonfire Sebastian and everyone else had ever seen.

With Sebastian's help Ralph held the flaming torch, and the two of them went steadily round the great pile of wood, lighting it in the eight evenly-spaced places where oil-soaked kindling had been placed. The crowd waited for the flames to take hold, and suddenly they did and roared up into the sky. A great cheer went up. The flames lit all their faces, good and bad, young and old, friendly and hostile, plain and beautiful, joyous and sad. From the loud-speaker system boisterous brass-band music blared forth, and then the music was stopped while a voice announced that the beer tent was open and the jacket potatoes would be brought round shortly.

Muriel had tears in her eyes. Her heart had nearly burst with pleasure when she saw Sebastian helping Ralph. She felt so proud of Ralph. So proud. Two Templetons lighting the fire. How fitting. Things did have a way of working out. She pulled her wool hat a little closer about her ears. She'd forgotten how sharply the wind blew straight across this open field. Her jacket potato held in her gloved hands, Muriel went to find Ralph.

Pat still hadn't found the rest of her family. She'd been looking for them before the bonfire had been lit and still hadn't made contact. She just hoped Michelle was OK. The girl was so confident, like as not she'd wandered off. Pat didn't like the skin of jacket potatoes, so she found a convenient bush and popped her skin behind there, content in the thought that a badger or a fox might be glad to eat it during the night.

'Caught in the act. What you up to?'

Pat jumped and spun round to see who it was.

'You stupid thing, Barry. Gave me the shock of mi life, you did.' Pat pressed her hand to her heart.

'Pleased with yer kitchen, are you? Put a lot of work into it, I have. I bet you'll be cooking some real nice meals in there, and I thought that bit of blank wall near the door yer could have a table and chairs. Nice warm kitchen to eat yer porridge in on a morning.'

'Well, there's one thing for certain, *you* won't be eating *your* porridge in there.'

'Aw! Pat! I'm cut to the quick. We could make a right go of it, you and me!'

He tried encircling her with his arms, but she gave him a hefty push on his chest. 'Daft thing you are. Get off with yer. You've been drinking!'

'I haven't! It's you, yer get my blood racing! Don't send me packing. We'll go for a drink in the beer tent and toast your good luck. Right?'

Why not? Pat argued to herself. 'Right, yer on.'

'Tuck yer arm in mine, don't want yer tumbling on this rough grass before you've even had a drink.' The first person they met was Venetia, wending her way back to the Big House. Venetia winked and gave Pat the thumbs-up. How embarrassing. Then she thought, who cares?

Peter and Caroline had got separated again. Beth was tired and fractious and obviously wasn't going to stay awake long enough to see the fireworks. 'Harriet! Have you seen my dear wife anywhere?'

Flick spoke before Harriet could reply. 'Wasn't Sebastian lucky to get chosen to light the bonfire, Mr Harris? I wish it had been me. Are you staying for the fireworks? I am. I'm having a lovely time, are you, Mr Harris?'

'I am indeed, Flick. I'm glad you're well enough to come tonight. Don't overtire yourself, will you?'

'Daddy says I'm almost A1 at Lloyd's now. So no, I'm not tired. Dr Harris is in the marquee, we've just left her there.'

Harriet laughed. 'When this daughter of mine allows me to get a word in, she's looking for you because Alex is tired and she's wanting to go home.'

'Right, I'll head for the marquee, then. Hope the rest of the evening goes well.' He waved and turned to go, but was stopped by Sheila Bissett. With her was a tall girl, a feminine edition of Ronald Bissett.

Sheila, bubbling with pride, introduced her daughter. 'Oh Rector, this is my daughter Bianca, you've never met, have you? She's come back home to live with us. Bianca, this is Peter Harris, our rector.' Bianca held out her hand to shake Peter's. He changed Beth over to his other arm and shook hands saying, 'Welcome to Turnham Malpas, Bianca. Nice to meet you. You've got a new job, then, somewhere close?'

'No, not yet. The bank where I worked was down-graded, someone had to go and it was a case of last in, first out. I've got various feelers out, so I'm hoping to get somewhere shortly. Mother tells me you have a very vigorous choir at the church. I'm a choral singer, sang Verdi's *Requiem* only last month. I should love the opportunity of singing in the church choir.'

Peter, never wishing to turn down an offer of help in the church, hesitated a moment before replying. It was all male, and the choir master intended it staying that way.

'I should have to speak with the choir master, he prefers an all male choir, and the St Thomas à Becket choir has been all male since time immemorial . . . so I'm afraid . . .'

'Surely you're not going to exclude me on the basis of sex?' Bianca's dark eyes began to spark. There was something about the way she hesitated before she said 'sex' which made Peter feel uncomfortable.

'Oh, no, no certainly not on that basis. I wouldn't like to be thought old-fashioned, but he is in charge not me, but I will have a word with him.'

'I have very good secretarial skills, so while I'm at a loose end perhaps I could do some work for you?'

Sheila decided to put a word in for Bianca. 'You'd be pleased for some help, wouldn't you, Peter? You've got excellent computer skills, haven't you, dear?' Bianca, not taking her eyes from Peter's face, nodded and smiled. Pressing the matter further, Sheila continued. 'You have a computer in your study, haven't you, Peter?'

'Good evening.' They hadn't heard Caroline approaching. She'd been listening to the conversation and had decided to interrupt. 'Sheila. Bianca.' She nodded her head in greeting. 'Nice to meet you. I'm Peter's wife, Caroline. I wonder if you would mind awfully if Peter and I took the children home? They're both very tired and I think they're going to have the screaming abdabs once the fireworks start. Perhaps you could discuss your contribution to the parish another day. I really am anxious to leave.'

Bianca surveyed Caroline. She noted the expensive suede jacket, the well cut trousers, the Jaeger scarf at her neck, the air of authority. Caroline observed Bianca's bleached hair, her strong features, and she recognised the hungry speculative look of a woman reaching thirty and still without a man of her own, and desperately wanting one.

Peter, a little surprised by Caroline's manner, agreed they needed to leave. 'I'll think about what you've suggested and let you know. Nice to have met you. Enjoy the rest of the evening, won't you? Goodnight.'

'Goodnight, Rector, 'night, Dr Harris.' Sheila and Bianca waved as the rectory party left.

Out of their hearing Peter said, 'You were rather abrupt, darling.' By the light of Caroline's torch they crossed the field towards their car.

'Sheila Bissett and I will never get on. The woman thoroughly irritates me. If that Bianca wants to sing in the choir, it will take all your diplomatic talents, believe me, to achieve a result.'

'I know, but I couldn't say no straight out, could I?'

'You're too kind and I love you for it. I can't spot the car. Where did we leave it? Oh, there it is. Perhaps not, but be warned. Open the door quickly, darling, Alex is getting awfully heavy, I think he's already fallen asleep. Predatory females are the last thing an attractive rector needs.'

They drove home in silence. Peter pulled up outside the rectory, switched off the engine, and turned to look at Caroline. 'My darling girl, you may well be right. I simply didn't notice. I don't need to say, do I, that I shall do everything in my power to keep the woman at arm's length?'

'Just watch your step. Occupational hazard, I'm afraid. Extraordinarily uncanny, how like her father she is in her looks. Come on, let's get the children to bed.'

By the time the firework display was over Jimbo was shattered. It had been a busy Saturday in the Store, and the organisation of the display had been more taxing than he had anticipated. Clearing up had to be left until Sunday, and he was glad. Rhett Wright and Dean Duckett were lined up to help clear away first thing Sunday. He wasn't too sure about Rhett. There seemed to be something odd about him. But if he did a good job then Jimbo decided he wouldn't complain. He collected Harriet and the baby, Flick, who was looking as shattered as he felt, and the two boys, and they went into the Big House to say their goodbyes and thank yous to Mr Fitch.

He was standing talking to Ralph, Muriel and Sadie. As soon as Mr Fitch saw Jimbo he broke off his conversation and went across to speak to him.

'Charter-Plackett! Brilliant display. Brilliant! Thank you very much indeed. Send your invoice in and it shall be paid immediately. Now, children, you've got your toffee apples I see?'

The children thanked him. He picked up a cardboard box. 'Look, I've some spare ones here in the box. Why not take an extra one home, each of you? Would you like that?'

The three children said in unison, 'Yes, please, Mr Fitch,' and helped themselves from the box he was holding.

'Clever husband you have, Harriet. When I heard what he'd done, left the bank and opted for a village shop, I thought, what a fool. But maybe he isn't as much of a fool as I thought! I'm quite taking to this country life.'

Harriet thanked him and, making her apologies, shepherded the children out. Frances was sleeping in her pram and Mr Fitch pulled back the blanket and took a peep at her. His face softened. He patted her arm, said, 'Goodnight, young lady,' and went back to Ralph and Muriel.

'Now, have the three of you time for a drink in my flat before you go?'

They followed him up the stairs and along the corridors to his flat. When he'd settled the two ladies with their drinks he handed Ralph his whisky, and as he did so Mr Fitch said, 'I've a proposition to make to you, Ralph. I should like to own some land around here — myself that is, not my company. These houses you're going to build. Now you've got planning permission, I wondered if you might be interested in selling the remainder of the land to me. Just the rest of the field, not the land the houses will be on. What do you say? I'll give you above the market valuation.'

Ralph was so staggered by his unexpected proposal that for a moment he was speechless.

Muriel answered indignantly. 'Certainly not! I wouldn't agree. It's Ralph's. It's ours. I won't allow it.'

Mr Fitch looked at Muriel and said, 'It's a joint venture then, is it?'

'Oh yes, it is.'

'I can't tempt *you* with money then? Not even above-market valuation? Surely it will tempt you, just a teeny little bit?'

'No, it won't. Will it, Ralph?'

Having collected his wits, Ralph ignored Muriel's question and asked Mr Fitch what he proposed to do with it; if he knew what he wanted it for he might, just might, be tempted. Muriel fumed. Mr Fitch smiled a little and replied, 'My ideas are not for public scrutiny yet. Suffice to say I want it and I'm willing to pay well for it. Now what do you say?'

'On the face of it, the offer is very tempting. Selling you the land would help finance the building of the houses, but I would want a good price, believe me, oh yes, a very good price. One can't afford to turn down a good offer, can one? I could well be tempted. Oh yes! I certainly could. Most definitely.'

Mr Fitch laughed triumphantly and thumped his fist against the palm of his other hand. 'Ha! I knew you'd see common sense.'

Muriel began to tremble with anger. She kept a tight grip on herself; after her last exhibition in front of Mr Fitch she daren't take any risks with her temper. But wait till she got Ralph home.

Ralph asked, 'What do you want to use it for?'

'As I've already said, I'm not disclosing that for the moment.'

Sadie interrupted their discussion. 'You know full well what you want to do with it Craddock, for heaven's sake stop playing the business magnate and be honest for once.'

Mr Fitch's lips tightened into a straight line. He sometimes felt Sadie had too much to say for herself.

Ralph pressed on with what he wished to say. 'The use to which my land is put is of paramount importance to me. If I'm not told what you will use it for I simply will not sell, no matter how much you offer. What's more, when I think about it, I couldn't trust you not to do something which would spoil the whole village, and this village of ours takes precedence over any get-rich-quick schemes you might care to come up with.' He calmly put down his glass and, slowly taking a cigar case from his pocket, nonchalantly selected one and then asked, 'Do you mind if I smoke?' The others shook their heads and watched him light it.

Mr Fitch, exasperated by his attitude, permitted his anger to break through his iron control. 'Hah! You country gentry think you own the world. I'm sorry, but it's laughable.'

'I do own the world. Round here, that is.'

'Well, I have to say I'm here to stay and I intend to buy up every cottage that becomes available, every piece of land I can. I love it around here, I really feel as though I've "come home".'

'Indeed! That's good! I'm glad you love it, I do too and no

one can stop you buying up houses and land. But there's one thing you won't buy and that is their hearts. They're mine!' He stretched wide the fingers of his upturned right hand and then, tensing his fingers, slowly closed them as though encompassing the entire village in his grasp. He held up his clenched fist to Mr Fitch. 'Mine! You can't buy their love and loyalty, they have to be earned over the years. And think on this, most of them only came tonight because they knew *I'd* agreed to come.' Ralph refrained from smiling triumphantly. He stood up. 'Now, Muriel, you must be ready to leave, I know I am. Thank you, Craddock, for a lovely evening. Very generous of you. Very. Goodnight, Sadie.'

Mr Fitch stood up when Muriel rose to her feet. He shook her hand and said, 'Well, I'm sorry you won't sell, very sorry. Sleep on it. You might change your mind. I can always live in hope!' He smiled pleadingly at her and then offered to see them to the main door. Ralph refused his courtesy. 'No thanks, Craddock. I actually do know my way out.' As the door to the flat closed behind them they heard Sadie say 'Touché!' and burst into peals of laughter. Ralph took Muriel's hand in his and led her along the corridors and down the staircase into the hall. He opened the main door and they stood looking out at the winter sky, enjoying the now frosty air and watching the glowing remnants of the bonfire across the field. Ralph blew a cloud of cigar smoke into the air and followed it with his eyes as it disappeared.

'Oh Ralph! You were wonderful! I'm so proud of you. To my shame, for one dreadful minute I really thought you *were* going to sell it to him.'

'He won't give up easily. But Fitch is not getting it. That land is the only land I own. Arthur Prior owns more than me. The years ahead could be very interesting, I'm looking forward to the challenge.'

He closed the door behind them and by the light of Muriel's torch they went down the neglected path to the gate in the churchyard wall, down the church path, out of the lych gate past Willie Bigg's and the rectory, and on to home.